DEADLY DISEASES AND EPIDEMICS

CHOLERA

DEADLY DISEASES AND EPIDEMICS

CHOLERA

William Coleman

CONSULTING EDITOR
I. Edward Alcamo
Distinguished Teaching Professor of Microbiology,
SUNY Farmingdale

FOREWORD BY
David Heymann
World Health Organization

CHELSEA HOUSE
P U B L I S H E R S
A Haights Cross Communications Company
Philadelphia

Dedication

We dedicate the books in the DEADLY DISEASES AND EPIDEMICS series to Ed Alcamo, whose wit, charm, intelligence, and commitment to biology education were second to none.

CHELSEA HOUSE PUBLISHERS

VP, NEW PRODUCT DEVELOPMENT Sally Cheney
DIRECTOR OF PRODUCTION Kim Shinners
CREATIVE MANAGER Takeshi Takahashi
MANUFACTURING MANAGER Diann Grasse

Staff for Cholera

ASSOCIATE EDITOR Beth Reger
ASSISTANT EDITOR Kate Sullivan
PRODUCTION EDITOR Jamie Winkler
PHOTO EDITOR Sarah Bloom
SERIES DESIGNER Terry Mallon
COVER DESIGNER Takeshi Takahashi
LAYOUT 21st Century Publishing and Communications, Inc.

A Haights Cross Communications ⌐ Company

http://www.chelseahouse.com

First Printing

1 3 5 7 9 8 6 4 2

Library of Congress Cataloging-in-Publication Data

Coleman, William, 1934–
    Cholera / William Coleman.
        p. cm.—(Deadly diseases and epidemics)
Includes index.
    ISBN 0-7910-7303-3
    1. Cholera—Juvenile literature. [1. Cholera.] I. Title. II. Series.
RC126.C695 2003
616.9'32—dc21

2002155048

Table of Contents

Foreword

In the 1960s, infectious diseases—which had terrorized generations—were tamed. Building on a century of discoveries, the leading killers of Americans both young and old were being prevented with new vaccines or cured with new medicines. The risk of death from pneumonia, tuberculosis, meningitis, influenza, whooping cough and diphtheria declined dramatically. New vaccines lifted the fear that summer would bring polio and a global campaign was approaching the global eradication of smallpox. New pesticides like DDT cleared mosquitoes from homes and fields, thus reducing the incidence of malaria which was present in the southern United States and a leading killer of children worldwide. New technologies produced safe drinking water and removed the risk of cholera and other water-borne diseases. Science seemed unstoppable. Disease seemed destined to almost disappear.

But the euphoria of the 1960s has evaporated.

Microbes fight back. Those causing diseases like TB and malaria evolved resistance to cheap and effective drugs. The mosquito evolved the ability to defuse pesticides. New diseases emerged including AIDS, Legionnaires, and Lyme disease. And diseases which have not been seen in decades re-emerge, as the hantavirus did in the Navajo Nation in 1993. Technology itself actually created new health risks. The global transportation network, for example, meant that diseases like West Nile virus could spread beyond isolated regions in distant countries and quickly become global threats. Even modern public health protections sometimes failed, as they did in Milwaukee, Wisconsin in 1993 which resulted in 400,000 cases of the digestive system illness cryptosporidiosis. And, more recently, the threat from smallpox, a disease completely eradicated, has returned along with other potential bioterrorism weapons such as anthrax.

The lesson is that the fight against infectious diseases will never end.

In this constant struggle against disease we as individuals have a weapon that does not require vaccines or drugs, the warehouse of knowledge. We learn from the history of science that "modern" beliefs can be wrong. In this series of books, for example, you will learn that diseases like syphilis were once thought to be caused by eating potatoes. The invention of the microscope set science on the right path. There are more positive lessons from history. For example, smallpox was eliminated by vaccinating everyone who had come in contact with an infected person. This "ring" approach to controlling smallpox is still the preferred method for confronting a smallpox outbreak should the disease be intentionally reintroduced.

At the same time, we are constantly adding new drugs, new vaccines, and new information to the warehouse. Recently, the entire human genome was decoded. So too was the genome of the parasite that causes malaria. Perhaps by looking at the microbe and the victim through the lens of genetics we will to be able to discover new ways of fighting malaria, still the leading killer of children in many countries.

Because of the knowledge gained about such diseases as AIDS, entire new classes of anti-retroviral drugs have been developed. But resistance to all these drugs has already been detected, so we know that AIDS drug development must continue.

Education, experimentation and the discoveries which grow out of them are the best tools to protect health. Opening this book may put you on the path of discovery. I hope so, because new vaccines, new antibiotics, new technologies and, most importantly, new scientists are needed now more than ever if we are to remain on the winning side of this struggle with microbes.

David Heymann
Executive Director
Communicable Diseases Section
World Health Organization
Geneva, Switzerland

1

Discovering Cholera

What is cholera? Cholera is the term used to describe a specific gastrointestinal disease as well as the bacterium which causes that disease. In this case, the disease was known long before the **microorganism** that causes it was even recognized. To understand this, it is necessary to go back through history.

THE GERM THEORY OF DISEASE

Microorganisms were not widely recognized as the causes of many diseases until late in the nineteenth century. However, some early scientists did propose that living organisms caused illnesses. The Italian physician Girolamo Fracastoro (ca. 1478–1553) spoke of "seeds" or "germs" of disease. Translations of Fracastoro's Latin writings indicate that he may have surmised that these "seeds" were alive. This is the earliest known written record of the **Germ Theory of Disease** – i.e., the concept that microorganisms cause some diseases. This concept was neglected for many years, however.

Over 300 years later, Agostino Bassi (1773–1856) described a disease of silkworms known as *muscardine* as being the result of a fungal infection of the worms. He could see the **fungus** as white, powdery material on silkworm eggs. It was identified as a fungus of the genus *Botrytis*. A botanist of the day confirmed this identification and named the fungus *Botrytis bassiana* in honor of Agostino Bassi.

LOUIS PASTEUR AND ROBERT KOCH

In the mid-nineteenth century the famous French scientist Louis Pasteur (1822–1895) had proven that microorganisms do not arise spontaneously.

His classic, simplistic, and ingenious experiment was to design a flask with an S-shaped curve in its neck. The curve trapped microorganisms that were present in the air before they could reach the main part of the flask. He filled the flasks with broth, heated them, and then allowed them to cool. In previous experiments using flasks without the S-shaped neck, microorganisms would grow in the broth. This did not occur in Pasteur's experiments. Critics stated that a "vital force" had been removed from the air by heating, so the microorganisms could not grow. Pasteur's flasks allowed the air to have access to the heated broth, defusing this argument. His cooled flasks did not become spoiled with bacterial growth because the microorganisms in the air had no means to ascend the tube leading to the broth once they were trapped in the dip, or curve, of the S-shaped flask. Pasteur went on to show that when he broke the spout of the flask, thereby destroying the S-shaped spout with the dip in it, the bacteria present in the air quickly grew in the broth. This experiment established once and for all that microorganisms do not arise spontaneously. They can, however, be grown in laboratories just like any other living thing.

In addition to this landmark experiment, Pasteur went on to make numerous contributions to understanding microorganisms. Among his many interests, Pasteur reexamined the problems of silkworm infection, which had been studied by Bassi so many years before, even though he was unaware of Bassi's work. Pasteur's efforts were sparked by his interest in the more general question of the microbial origins of infections. He studied infections in higher animals as a result of these efforts. This occurred in the late 1800s, a golden era in microbiology. Pasteur, along with his main competitor, the German scientist Robert Koch (1843–1910), studied numerous microorganisms and the effects they caused, including diseases.

Robert Koch (Figure 1.1) was the first person to show that a specific microbe can cause an infectious disease in a higher animal. He isolated the bacterium that causes tuberculosis in 1882. A year later, he published a report describing the bacterium that causes the disease cholera. This microorganism is called *Vibrio cholerae*. How was Koch able to isolate this one microorganism and associate it with cases of the infection?

In order to isolate and identify *Vibrio cholerae*, Koch had to grow this microorganism free from all other microorganisms. A microorganism grown in this manner is called a **pure culture** of a microorganism. In addition, Kock had to develop a growth medium, as well as a technique to separate the many thousands of microbes in a sample so that just one microbe could grow, dividing repeatedly to form visible growth. This growth is referred to as a **colony** of a specific bacterium.

KOCH'S TECHNIQUES
FOR THE STUDY OF MICROBES

Koch first made a growth **medium** using 2.5 to 5 percent gelatin (a protein obtained from the tendons of animals) in a nutrient soup. He spread the medium on a glass slide and allowed it to solidify at room temperature. Next, he sterilized a metal wire by heating it in a flame. When the wire cooled, Koch dipped it into the area where the bacteria were located, and used the wire to draw a line onto the solid medium on the slide. He repeated this process many times, as illustrated in Figure 1.2.

Koch then placed the slide in a warm incubator. After the bacteria had grown on the medium, the slide was removed for observation. The first streaks on the slide contained many microbes. Each subsequent streak had fewer microbes. Eventually, only single cells (instead of large clumps) grew in each area. After the cells had been allowed to grow overnight, the single cells had formed colonies (individual microbes that have divided repeatedly to form a group of cells visible to the

Figure 1.1. Robert Koch, pictured here, discovered that certain microorganisms can cause specific diseases. Along with studying anthrax and cholera, his rules for proving that a microorganism causes disease has become standard in the practice of microbiology today. These rules are known as Koch's postulates.

naked eye) about 1–2 millimeters in diameter. Each colony was a **clone**, a pure culture of identical cells.

Koch had problems with the use of gelatin in this procedure. Many microorganisms could degrade the gelatin protein, turning the medium to mush. In addition, gelatin melts at

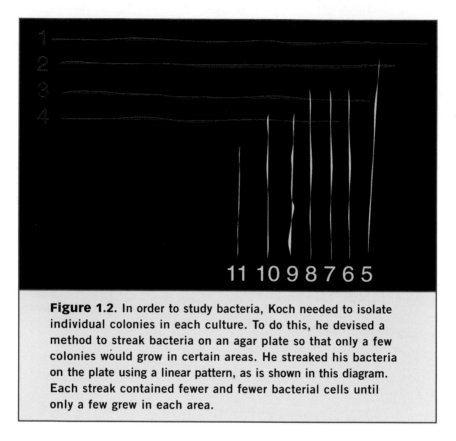

Figure 1.2. In order to study bacteria, Koch needed to isolate individual colonies in each culture. To do this, he devised a method to streak bacteria on an agar plate so that only a few colonies would grow in certain areas. He streaked his bacteria on the plate using a linear pattern, as is shown in this diagram. Each streak contained fewer and fewer bacterial cells until only a few grew in each area.

body temperature, the very temperature which is most likely to support the growth of an infectious microorganism. A turn of events, which is, by now, a legend, occurred. The wife of one of Koch's co-workers suggested using a cooking additive for the growth medium instead of gelatin. The additive was called **agar**. She had learned from a Dutch friend that this substance was often used in preparing jellies and soups in Java (a former Dutch colony and now part of Indonesia). Agar is dried seaweed (Genus and species: *Agar agar*) which can be ground and dissolved when heated in water. It remains in a liquid form for some hours at 50°C, and it solidifies below 42°C. Koch recognized that agar provided a better growth medium than gelatin for the isolation of pure cultures. It remains in use today.

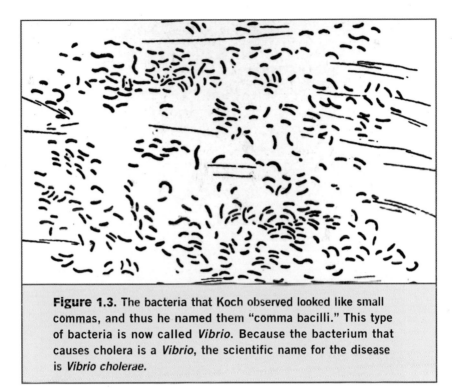

Figure 1.3. The bacteria that Koch observed looked like small commas, and thus he named them "comma bacilli." This type of bacteria is now called *Vibrio*. Because the bacterium that causes cholera is a *Vibrio*, the scientific name for the disease is *Vibrio cholerae*.

Another legacy of Koch's early lab is the glass dish that was developed by an assistant of Koch, R. J. Petri. The Petri dish is standard today in the study of microorganisms. One can see colonies without removing the glass cover of the dish. The agar medium can be varied while it is still liquid, then poured into Petri dishes rather than spread onto glass slides, as Koch had done originally.

The **streak plate method** for the isolation of pure cultures of bacteria is also standard today. These methods had to be developed before Koch could establish that microorganisms caused cholera and other diseases. When he first observed the microbes he isolated, they appeared as small commas, so he referred to them as "comma bacilli" (Figure 1.3). Another name for this curved rod-shaped bacterium is a *vibrio* (Figure 1.4). Hence, the official name for this microorganism is *Vibrio cholerae*.

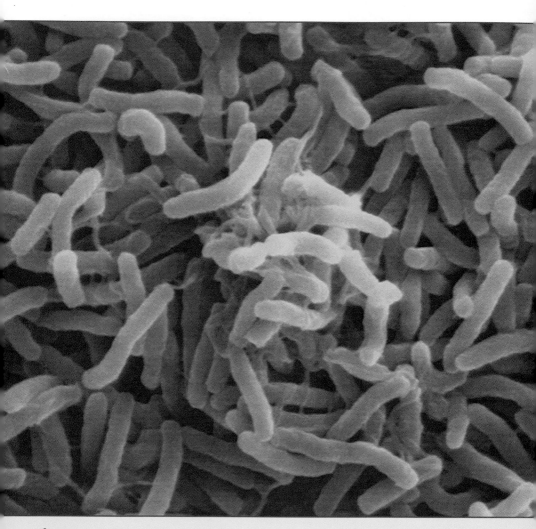

Figure 1.4. This electron micrograph shows the curved and spiral nature of the *Vibrio* bacteria. Koch found that older cultures contained more spiral-shaped vibrios, while newer cultures contained more comma-shaped bacteria.

KOCH'S POSTULATES

Not content merely to observe a microbe present in an infected individual, Koch established guidelines for proving that a microbe causes a particular infection. These guidelines are called "Koch's Postulates" and are still used today as standards for establishing proof of infection. They are, in brief:

1. The microbe has to be present in every case of the disease.

2. The microbe has to be isolated from the patient and grown in pure culture.

3. When the purified microorganism is inoculated into a healthy susceptible host, the same disease results.

4. Once again, the same microbe must be isolated from the host infected with the microbe.

Koch's remarkable contributions were landmarks to the fields of microbiology, medicine, and scientific study in general. He received the Nobel Prize in Medicine in 1905 for his work related to tuberculosis; moreover, his techniques and protocols for laboratory investigation are still in use today.

2

Properties of *Vibrio cholerae*

Koch discovered that *Vibrio cholerae* causes cholera. But how is this organism unique? Does it resemble other microorganisms that cause similar diseases? How is it different? How can this information help isolate *Vibrio cholerae* from the thousands of other microorganisms that inhabit the human body at any given time?

KOCH'S FIRST LOOK

Koch headed a commission established by the German government to study cholera in Egypt and India. His discovery of the "comma bacillus" in a large number of cases of the disease indicated that a bacillus of this same shape was probably present every time. In addition, Koch was able to see firsthand the transmittal of the disease and subsequent infection by the bacilli when two of his laboratory assistants became seriously ill and nearly died after drinking the tainted water.

What Koch saw in his study of *Vibrio cholerae* was a small, curved rod, ranging in length from one to two microns, which is only one or two millionth of a meter. The microbes curved in various ways: some were only slightly bent while others had spirals of one or two turns that looked like corkscrews. The bacterium was also actively **motile**. When Koch stained the bacteria with a special stain, he could see that each organism contained a single polar flagellum, or tail. The organism did not appear to form spores. Young cultures contained more comma-shaped forms while the spiral forms of the microbe dominated older

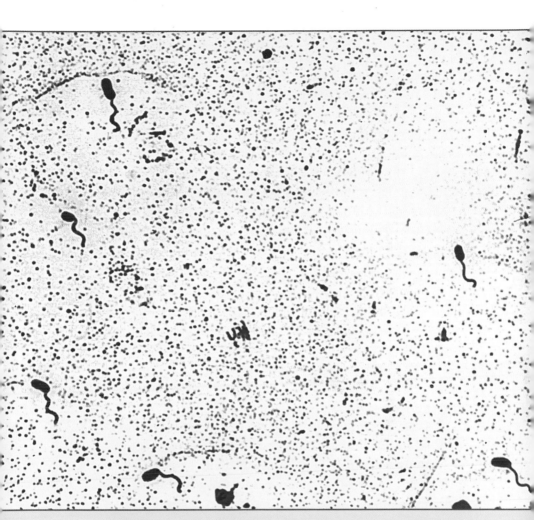

Figure 2.1. A test called the Gram stain reaction allows scientists to differentiate between different types of bacteria. The cholera bacillus is considered Gram negative because it takes up the pink counterstain safranin. These cells are pink because they are Gram negative.

cultures. It is now known that if the microbe is grown in the laboratory and does not pass through an animal body, the microbes tend to lose their curvature entirely. Koch also observed that the microorganism was decolorized when using the **Gram stain reaction**.

LOOKING AT THE CHOLERA BACILLUS TODAY

Today, *Vibrio cholerae* is classified as Gram negative, since it decolorizes after staining with crystal violet but takes up the **counterstain** safranin (Figure 2.1).

The cholera bacillus is fairly easy to grow in the laboratory. It will grow in most common laboratory media such as nutrient broth or nutrient agar but will also grow on meat extracts. The organism prefers media that is moderately alkaline, but this is not essential since it will also tolerate mild acidity. Small, strongly refracting yellowish-gray colonies appear after 24 hours of growth on gelatin plates. However, the gelatin liquifies as the organism continues to grow. The colonies are coarsely granular with uneven edges (due to the liquefaction of the gelatin). In gelatin stab cultures, liquefaction begins at the top, leading to a funnel-shaped pattern of gelatin liquification. This ability to attack gelatin is lost in old strains of the bacterium which have been grown artificially in the laboratory for long periods.

On agar plates, grayish and opalescent colonies appear within 18 to 24 hours. The fact that *Vibrio cholerae* is opalescent helps in the identification and isolation of these microorganisms from patients, because other bacteria likely to appear in feces are not opalescent. In addition, the bacillus can liquify coagulated blood serum and also grow on starch, appearing as a brownish coarse growth. The cholera bacillus grows abundantly on alkaline peptone medium. This trait is particularly helpful when a scientist needs to isolate the microorganism from mixed samples, such as a fecal specimen. The cholera bacilli also produce a crystalline compound called indole, which also helps with identification.

Vibrio species can grow at a broad temperature range (from 18°C to 37°C) on a variety of simple media, aerobically or anaerobically. Therefore, the bacterium is described as **aerobic** and **facultatively anaerobic**. It grows optimally at 37.5°C, which is normal human body temperature. The microorganism has a positive oxidase reaction which means that is has the enzyme cytochrome oxidase, a key enzyme in aerobic metabolism.

Cholera bacteria can live about three or four days when frozen in ice. They die immediately when heated to boiling (100°C). They are killed within an hour at a temperature of 60°C. Drying will also kill the cells in a short period of time. When in impure water, in food, on cloth, or other complex environmental conditions, they may live for many days. Dilute solutions of common disinfectants destroy these bacteria after exposure for a few minutes.

ISOLATING CHOLERA BACILLI FROM PATIENTS

The properties of *Vibrio cholerae* discussed in the previous section are important for the isolation and identification of the cholera bacillus from patient specimens. The procedures for examination of **stool specimens** (fecal material) from patients outline methods to test for: 1) animal parasites, 2) routine examinations for microorganisms, and finally 3) examinations for special or unusual cases. The search for cholera bacilli falls into this third category, since it is not an ordinary or suspected disease in the United States. However, in areas where the bacillus is more commonly observed, the procedures for isolating and identifying cholera bacilli are undoubtedly routine. If a virus is suspected, **tissue culture** and electron microscopy methods are also used in an attempt to identify the offending microorganism. Sample specimens from special cases are placed in culture medium at 22°C, inoculated into alkaline peptone water which will help to increase the number of bacilli in the sample, and streaked thiosulfate-citrate-bile salt-sucrose (TCBS) medium plates. TCBS plates also contain a bromothymol blue indicator which helps to identify colonies. Microorganisms that do not ferment sucrose grow best on TCBS medium

Figure 2.2. Scientists grow bacteria such as *Vibrio cholerae* on agar plates. Agar is a gelatin-like substance that solidifies at 42°C. In this picture, a scientist streaks cells on an agar plate using a method similar to the once that was pioneered by Robert Koch. The cells will grow on the media and become colonies that are visible to the naked eye.

and produce blue-green colonies. Because *Vibrio cholerae* does ferment sucrose, it will produce tallow-colored colonies on this medium. The fermentation process involves the formation of acid from sucrose, and the acid reacts with bromothymol blue, resulting in a color change. The **bile salts** in this medium and the high pH (8.6) prevent the growth of other bacteria associated with the gastrointestinal tract. Medically important microorganisms which do not ferment sucrose include *Vibrio parahaemolyticus, Aeromonas* spp. (species) and *Plesiomonas* spp. These are the non-cholera food poisoning vibrios, which are related to *Vibrio cholera*, yet distinct. Cholera bacilli in fresh stool samples will also have a characteristic darting mobility, which aids in the identification of the microorganism.

Having proceeded this far, one might think that the search for the cholera bacillus in a patient sample is complete. This is true, yet it is still necessary to identify what type of strain is present, as many different strains of the bacillus exist. The strains can be identified by matching them to antibodies that are formed against each different type. In order to understand this process, one must examine the structural variations which define each of the strains.

THE CHOLERA BACILLUS AS A PROKARYOTE OF THE DOMAIN BACTERIA

All life forms are either **prokaryotes** or **eukaryotes**. Eukaryotic cells contain a nucleus and other membrane-bound organelles. The DNA of the cell is contained on chromosomes which are located within the nucleus. Animal, plant, and fungal cells are eukaryotes. Prokaryotes, on the other hand, are generally smaller in size, do not have a nucleus or membrane-bound organelles, and the DNA resides within the cytoplasm. Bacteria are prokaryotes.

Using special techniques to obtain the sequence of nucleic acid bases in the ribosomal RNA, scientists discovered that there are three distinct types of life forms on Earth. Two of these catergories, Archaea and Bacteria, are prokaryotes. Organisms in the Archaea group are thought to be the oldest life forms that still exist on earth. These microorganisms live in extreme places in our environment such as regions of high salt, high temperature, and places where methane can be formed. For this reason, Archaea microorganisms are often referred to as extremophiles. For example, the hot geyser pools in Yellowstone National Park, Wyoming, have yielded numerous high temperature-growing microorganisms (thermophiles). Microorganisms in the group Archaea differ from those in the group Bacteria in several ways. Archaea have a unique RNA sequence and a different cell wall composition, consisting of ether bonds in the lipids rather than ester bonds. Due to this cell wall difference, antibiotics that work against Archaea are different from those that will work against Bacteria. Often the antibiotics that act on eukaryotes will also act on Archaea, but not on Bacteria. Scientists have discovered that *Vibrio* organisms are part of the domain Bacteria.

The Gram stain procedure utilizes a primary stain, crystal violet, and a secondary stain, safranin. Cells are first treated with crystal violet, and then rinsed. Next, safranin is added. Cells that are considered Gram positive will retain the crystal violet dye even after they are rinsed. Gram negative cells will not retain the primary stain. Recall that Koch and others determined that *Vibrio cholerae* was Gram negative. Nearly 50 years later, scientists discovered that chemical differences in the cell walls of different cells leads to the distinction in staining characteristics.

Gram negative bacteria have an additional outer cell membrane layer. This outer layer is outside the cell wall polymer of N-acetylglucose and N-acetylglucosamine polysaccharide chains, a thin layer overlying the cell membrane. Both the outer and inner membranes are composed of lipid bilayers. However, the additional lipid bilayer in Gram negative bacteria necessitates the formation of protein structures (**porins**) which can help transport water-soluble materials into the bacterial cell. In contrast, Gram positive microorganisms have a thick layer of cell wall polymer above the single lipid bilayer cell membrane.

The outer membrane of a Gram negative bacterial cell contains numerous proteins and lipopolysaccharides. Each element has an important function. **Lipid A** is attached to the outermost layer of the membrane. A core polysaccharide is attached to Lipid A. Each core polysaccharide has a special side chain which varies from one species of Gram negative

THE GRAM STAIN REACTION

The Gram stain was developed by Christian Gram. This staining procedure differentiates bacteria into two categories, Gram positive and Gram negative. First, the microorganisms are attached to a glass slide and then stained with crystal violet dye. An iodine solution consisting of iodine and iodide ion is then applied to the bacteria. The crystal violet reacts with the iodine solution inside the bacterial cells. A complex of crystal violet and iodine forms. Next, the cells are treated with 95 percent ethyl alcohol solution. Some cells will retain the purple color after the alcohol treatment and are designated as Gram positive bacteria. Other cells will lose the purple color of the dye (the crystal violet-iodine complex washes out) and are considered Gram negative. Gram negative bacteria are then stained with safranin, which give them a contrasting light red color. Cholera bacilli are Gram negative.

Years later, it was discovered that there are fundamental structural differences between Gram negative and Gram positive bacteria. Gram positive bacteria have a thick cell wall surrounding the cell membrane. Gram negative bacteria have a cell membrane, a thin cell wall over that, and an additional lipid bilayer membrane outside the cell wall and facing the exterior of the cell. This additional lipid bilayer contains components that are unique for each species of Gram negative bacteria.

Gram positive and Gram negative bacteria have different properties and characteristics because of these distinctly different cell structures.

bacteria to another. This entire complex (the core polysaccharide and the side chain) is called a lipopolysaccharide (**LPS**). The LPS plus Lipid A is called an **endotoxin** because the complex is toxic to many different animals. Gram negative bacteria containing LPS without the Lipid A portions are non-toxic.

ANTIBODIES AS A RESPONSE TO THE OUTER STRUCTURES OF CHOLERA BACILLI

Like nearly all foreign invaders, the cholera bacilli will invoke an immune response from its host. Any substance that invokes an immune response is called an **antigen** and alerts the host organism to form antibodies. An **antibody** is a protein that attacks a specific foreign body. Early investigations by German microbiologists recognized two major types of antibodies that formed in response to bacteria like the cholera bacillus. One type of antibody could recognize the proteins of the flagella. The Germans used their word for film ("Hauch") to describe these antibodies. These microbes can move and were observed to form films across the surfaces of media. These became known as H antigens or flagellar antigens. The antibodies that formed against the rest of the cell were said to be "without film" ("ohne Hauch") and thus were designated O antigens. These are also referred to as somatic or cellular antigens, indicating that these are part of the main body or structure of the bacterial cells. The polar flagellum and fimbria of *Vibrio cholerae* can be seen using an electron microscope (Figure 2.3).

Using these techniques, scientists have discovered about 150 different strains of *Vibrio cholerae*. In addition to the classical cholera form, four important strains that will be discussed are *El Tor, Ogawa, Inaba,* and *Hikojima.* The cholera-causing bacteria are classified in **serotype** O1. Classical cholera possessing this somatic antigen was the only type with this

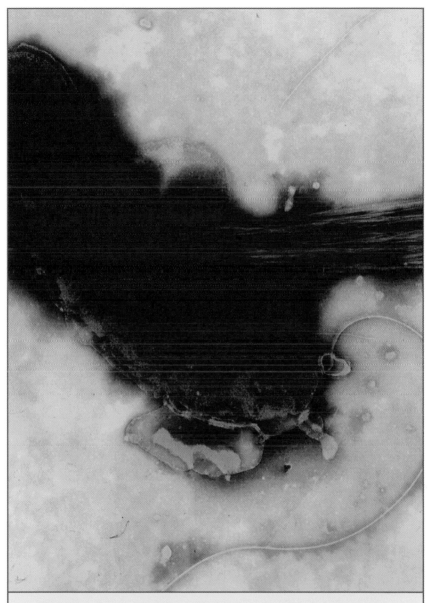

Figure 2-3. This electron micrograph shows the flagellum and fimbria of a *Vibrio cholerae* bacterium. The flagellum is a tail-like projection that helps the cell to move.

antigen until the discovery of the strain called El Tor. The El Tor strain was isolated from pilgrims at El Tor in the Sinai peninsula. This strain is capable of agglutinating red blood cells from chicks, and it is resistant to antibiotics generally used to treat classical cholera.

There are three different polysaccharides that have been found as part of the O1 antigen structure. These are indicated as types A, B, and C. The Ogawa strain has types A and B, the Inaba strain has types A and C, and a rare type has been found which has all three of these polysaccharides (Hikojima strain). They can be distinguished by using antibodies specific to each strain and by comparing reactions to the different bacterial strains. For example, antibodies to the Ogawa strain would react best when mixed with antibodies to the Ogawa bacillus. However, there would be some reaction with the Inaba strain, since it shares the A polysaccharide in the O1 antigen. The reaction of antigens and antibodies is usually observed by mixing antigens and antibodies on slides and observing agglutination (clumping) due to the large antigen-antibody complexes that form and precipitate from solution.

Patients react differently to the classical and the El Tor strains. Compared to the classical strain, diarrhea is short-lived in the El Tor strains. Patients infected with the El Tor strain often do not express symptoms but become **carriers** of the bacteria. Because of these and other biological differences, these strains which have the somatic antigen O1 are called **biotypes**. Strains that are distinguished by different immunological reactions (Ogawa, Inaba) are called **serotypes**. In 1992, a new serotype designated *O139 syn. Bengal* was isolated in India and Bangladesh.

Now, the identification of the cholera bacillus is complete. Performing **slide agglutination** tests on the microbes isolated from the stool specimen by growth on TCBS agar can indicate the specific serotype found. This is particularly important for tracking a specific type of cholera bacillus during epidemics.

However, one can not assume that all strains of *Vibrio cholerae* have been discovered. It is possible that new strains can form if current forms of the organism mutate. Should that happen, there are methods to identify, characterize, and hopefully develop appropriate treatments for the new strains.

3

Dr. Snow and Cholera

A CASE OF SUSPECTED CHOLERA:
Miners in Victorian England

In 1831 in Newcastle-upon-Tyne, England, a group of coal miners who had been perfectly fit and healthy in the morning returned from the mines profusely **defecating** (eliminating solid wastes) with abundant **diarrhea** (loose, watery, solid wastes). They were in a state of near exhaustion. Granted, their work in the mines was hard and the conditions grueling, but this could not explain the fact that soon most collapsed and died.

John Snow (Figure 3.1), then 18 years old and in his second year as apprentice to the local doctor at Newcastle-upon-Tyne, was sent to give the miners and their families any medical assistance that he could. Although Dr. Snow knew at once that the men were ill with cholera, there was little he could do for them. Cholera was familiar to the British from their visits to India, where it was common. The miners were in the same condition as people believed to be suffering from cholera in India.

After seven more years as an apprentice to several physicians, John Snow passed the medical examinations. At the age of 25, he set up practice as a physician and sold drugs and other medicines. He could have continued to practice medicine with no further education or medical degrees. For him, though, his present knowledge about infectious diseases was not enough. Most physicians of the day believed that cholera and other such infectious diseases were carried through "bad air." Dr. Snow did not agree. Furthermore, he was intrigued by many unanswered questions in the medical field and thus decided to study medicine further. He attended the college and the newly opened medical school at the University of London when he was 30 years old and graduated in 1844.

Figure 3.1. John Snow discovered the path of cholera transmission through his careful observation of the 1854 cholera epidemic in London. He was the first scientist to propose that cholera was transmitted through contaminated water.

Dr. Snow was aware of documented cases of cholera in India that dated as far back as 1789. However, it is likely that cholera existed in India before Europeans went there for regular visits. As travel between India and Europe increased, it is very likely that cholera followed them home. Because the first cases of cholera in England were thought to have originated in India, the disease was often called Asiatic cholera.

The following case study is presented to give an example of observations that piqued Dr. Snow's curiosity. Rather than draw conclusions from one such case, Dr. Snow accumulated information from many such case observations. This case and others helped him to develop his hypothesis that cholera is a communicable disease spread through water.

DR. SNOW'S DATA COLLECTION

Dr. Snow began to take a close look at case studies of cholera. One case, that of John Harnold, a seaman who in the autumn of 1848 arrived in London by steamer from Hamburg, Germany, was quite intriguing. Cholera was raging in Hamburg, and John Harnold was ill. He died of cholera within a few hours after the first symptoms appeared. Eight days later, a man who rented the room that Mr. Harnold had used also died of cholera. The doctor attending him, however, did not. Dr. Snow wanted to know why two men had died, yet the third had not. Many learned men of the day thought that diseases such as cholera were carried from one person to another through the air. Dr. Snow wanted to find out for sure.

Dr. Snow knew of many cases in which it seemed clear that the disease was carried from a sick person to a healthy person. He began to collect this information and keep careful records of these cases. Many of his medical colleagues also kept recods. From all his experiences both in treating patients and in examinations after death, he observed that the main part of the body affected by cholera was the **alimentary canal**, the part of the body responsible for digestion. He began to think that cholera might be spread through drinking water. Snow believed that this was the method of disease **communication**.

Dr. Snow formed the **hypothesis** that cholera is a communicable disease spread through water. Following the *scientific method* for problem solving, he continued his clinical observations, carefully collecting data which might prove his preliminary idea. However, the many clinical cases in which cholera had passed to a healthy person from a person who had been in contact with an infected individual did not prove or disprove his hypothesis. In some of these cases, the persons who became ill were near to but not in contact with the patient at all. Yet, some got cholera and some did not. Why was this so?

One outbreak was particularly telling. Rows of small cottages inhabited by poor people were separated by a single street in Horsleytown, England. The north side of the cottages was called Surrey Buildings, and the south side of the cottages was called Truscott's Court. During 1849, there were many cases of cholera in the Surrey Buildings but only two cases in Truscott's Court. Household wastewater was poured into a channel in front of the houses in both cases. The wastewater from the residents of the Surrey Buildings (and not Truscott's Court) reached the well which the residents used for drinking water. Furthermore, the two sets of buildings received the well water from different water companies.

Dr. Snow did not draw conclusions from any one case. Rather, he examined many cases and their extent, appearance, and geographical location before formulating any conclusions. In short, he was the first scientist to use methods of **epidemiology**, which are employed to this day.

DR. SNOW USES MAPS
TO HELP TRACK THE DISEASE

Outbreaks of cholera occurred regularly during the nineteenth century. In 1854, Dr. Snow reported one of the most severe outbreaks to date. In a period of three days, 127 people in the area of Broad Street in London died from the disease. Dr. Snow kept records of this **epidemic** by marking a street map of the area with the location of each of the cholera patients (Figures 3.2 and 3.3). He saw that there were more cases closer to the water pump, and the numbers of cases diminished at

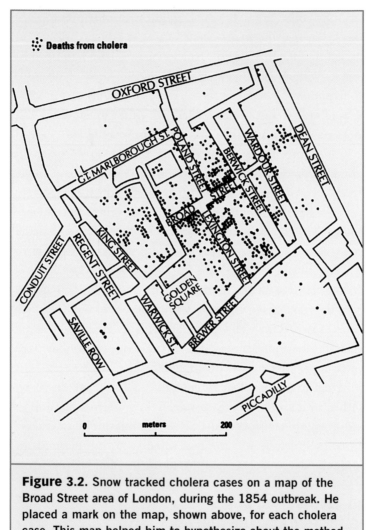

Figure 3.2. Snow tracked cholera cases on a map of the Broad Street area of London, during the 1854 outbreak. He placed a mark on the map, shown above, for each cholera case. This map helped him to hypothesize about the method of cholera transmission.

distances from the water pump. Sanitary conditions were similar in other areas of the neighborhood, but there were few or no cases of cholera in the vicinity of other water pumps. This convinced Dr. Snow that this cholera outbreak was the result of drinking water from the Broad Street water pump.

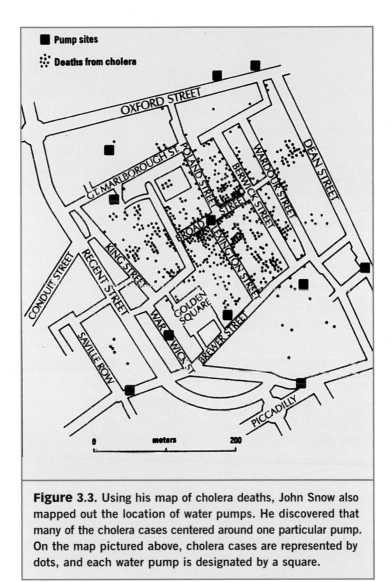

Figure 3.3. Using his map of cholera deaths, John Snow also mapped out the location of water pumps. He discovered that many of the cholera cases centered around one particular pump. On the map pictured above, cholera cases are represented by dots, and each water pump is designated by a square.

Dr. Snow also realized that some people who lived far from the city and Broad Street were dying of cholera even though they most likely did not use water from the Broad Street pump. In order to prove his theory that cholera was not "in the air," but in the water, he investigated one such case. A lady from

Hampstead, a suburb of the city of London, had died of cholera. Her son told Dr. Snow that she had not been in the vicinity of Broad Street for many months. This was truly puzzling. The water in the household was clear and had never been in contact with sewage. Dr. Snow began questioning members of the household, including the staff. One servant told him that the woman had a fondness for water drawn from the pump at Broad Street in London. The servant was sent to the Broad Street neighborhood every week to draw water from the pump and had done so during the time of the cholera epidemic. The woman, in turn, drank this water. This was the connection that Dr. Snow was looking for. The mystery surrounding cholera **transmission** had been solved.

Dr. Snow also realized that there were fewer cases of cholera in the area just east of the Broad Street pump (see Figure 3.2 and 3.3). Dr. Snow talked to the owners of a brewery located in this area and found that the workers at the brewery did not drink from the Broad Street pump because the owner of the brewery supplied beer for his workers. He assured Dr. Snow that these men drank beer and not water! This helped explain the lower numbers of cholera cases in that area of the city.

Dr. Snow realized that something had to be done to reduce the transmission of cholera in the area. He discussed the problem with the Board of Guardians of St. James's Parish, which had jurisdiction over the area of the Broad Street water pump. Snow told them that the pump was the source of the cholera in this latest epidemic, and he recommended that they shut it down. Very reluctantly, they heeded his advice to do so, and the pump handle was removed.

Although this particular epidemic may have already reached its peak and was beginning to wane by the time Dr. Snow convinced St. James's Parish to remove the pump handle, it is certain that his research prevented future infections from the Broad Street water pump. In later years, this set of observations has been referred to as the "Grand

Experiment" of Dr. Snow and has entered the realm of folklore in the history of medicine.

THE BEGINNINGS OF EPIDEMIOLOGY

Through his careful study of the Broad Street cholera epidemic as well as many other studies and observations, one can surmise that Dr. Snow founded the science of epidemiology. Epidemiology is the study of disease transmission, its incidence in a population, and methods of control and prevention. Even today, an important aspect of studying an epidemic is the accurate reporting of the location of infected individuals. Dr. Snow's contributions to the science of microbiology not only include an understanding of the way cholera is transmitted, but also invaluable tools for understanding infectious diseases within a population. His work led to the study of public health, and to this day we benefit from his legacy.

TRACKING EPIDEMICS

Did you know that satellites can track worldwide epidemics? Ocean height, turbidity, and sea surface temperature can be observed and photographed from above and have often been linked to emerging epidemics. By examining photographs from past years as well as the data giving the numbers of cholera cases during those years, it has been shown that there is an increase in the numbers of cholera cases when the sea surface temperature is elevated and the ocean height is high.

NASA scientists relate that this information connects changes in climate such as the El Niño effect to cholera outbreaks. They are continuing to gather information about increased growth of algae in seas and possible relationships to cholera epidemics.

http://geo.arc.nasa.gov/sge

4

Transmission and Epidemiology of Cholera

THE TRANSMISSION OF CHOLERA

As learned in Chapter 3, Dr. Snow successfully described the connection between water supply and cholera infections. He did this through careful observation of the location of disease sufferers and by adhering to the scientific method. This was the groundwork for many studies of epidemics and the spread of diseases. It is remarkable that Dr. Snow's insights came before scientists knew, or even accepted the fact, that cholera is caused by a microorganism.

It is known that cholera infection is a result of transmission from environmental contamination to an individual, or from one individual to another. Human beings are the only known natural host of *Vibrio cholerae*, the microorganism which causes cholera. Poor **sanitation** methods lead to the contamination of soil, food, or water with *Vibrio cholerae* bacilli from **feces**. The cycle of transmission is complete when a person becomes a carrier. Individuals who are recovering from the disease may feel better but they still carry the microorganism within their bodies. These people are known as *convalescent carriers*. People who harbor the microorganism but do not yet show signs and symptoms of the disease are called *incubatory carriers*. They are also important in the transmission cycle of cholera.

Experiments using volunteers have shown that a dose of 10^3 (1000) *Vibrio cholerae* cells are required to infect a person. These bacteria may come from contaminated water or from contaminated food, such as vegetables grown in human waste fertilizer. Cholera may also be spread directly from person to person. This often occurs when a cholera patient is being treated at home or when a cholera victim is being prepared for burial. *Vibrio cholerae* can survive on the body or clothing of a victim; thus the bacilli may be passed to anyone in close contact with the body. Because the disease causes profuse, watery diarrhea, cholera patients excrete many liters of fluid each day, and this fluid contains about 10^6 to 10^8 cholera bacteria per milliliter. Therefore, contact with cholera patients poses a considerable risk of infection.

Cholera bacteria can be killed by heat, but they survive in the cold. They can live for two or more weeks in food such as milk, cooked rice, and seafood. They are sensitive to acidity, but survive in alkaline environments. Thus, there are many opportunities for infection through food and drink.

THE HISTORY OF CHOLERA

Scholars do not entirely agree on the origin of the word "cholera." It has been suggested that the word cholera is derived from the Greek word for bile (cholera) and flow (rein). Others suggest that in Greek the word "cholera" (which can also be interpreted as "roof gutter") probably indicates symptoms of water flow like that after a heavy rain. Cholera has been documented several times throughout history. A disease with symptoms similar to those of cholera is described in Sanskrit documents dating from about 500 B.C. to 400 B.C. Cholera was described early in the sixteenth century by European arrivals to India. It was documented by a staff member of the explorer Vasco da Gama that 20,000 men died of cholera in the early 1500s.

Since 1817, researchers have documented cholera epidemics all across the world. A worldwide epidemic is called a **pandemic**. Other patterns of disease spread have also been observed for cholera. If the disease is present at a low, persistent level in a population, it is said to be **endemic**. The first cholera pandemic occurred as a result of wars between Persia and Turkey when soldiers were traveling between their native lands and could unknowingly carry the disease with them. The second pandemic is thought to have originated in Russia and spread to the Americas, reaching New York on June 23, 1832. The disease traveled to Philadelphia, and eventually to New Orleans. It was during this second pandemic, when it passed through London, that Dr. Snow made his observations that would ultimately connect water to cholera transmission.

Cholera first appeared in Chicago, Illinois in 1849 when it was brought to the city via a boat carrying immigrants. From this point on, cholera epidemics occurred regularly in the city. City officials attempted to improve sanitation by using water from nearby Lake Michigan rather than local wells which were often contaminated by sewage from the Chicago River. In 1867, the city opened a two-mile-long tunnel that carried water from the lake into the city. This further reduced the amount of sewage from the river into the local water supply.

NEW YORK: The 1892 Cholera Panic

By the 1890s, public awareness of cholera had grown significantly. In August 1892, emigrants from Hamburg, Germany, arrived in New York City. At that time, cholera was raging in Europe. Upon arrival, these ships were quarantined and steerage passengers were sent to special quarantine hospitals. Cabin passengers traveling first- and second-class were not allowed off the ship for 20 days. The passengers were not happy with this decision. They wanted to disembark right away because some of the workers on the ship were ill with cholera, and the passengers feared infection. The governor of New York decided to buy an unused hotel and the surrounding 120 acres of land in Babylon and Islip Town on Long Island for the quarantined passengers. The local residents felt threatened because they were afraid that they would catch the disease too. They took up weapons and threatened arson and other forms of violence if the governor allowed the boat passengers to stay in their towns. When the ship tried to dock, an angry mob of about 400 people stood waiting. They had sailed across the bay to the island where the hotel was located to confront the authorities. A State Supreme Court judge issued an injunction against the landing, and the mob went back home, satisfied. The National Guard and Naval Reserve were called in to keep peace. Eventually, a few of the quarantined passengers were allowed to disembark without incident.

This incident shows how the fear of infection can cause hysteria. Remember that this was during a time when little was known about this disease except that it made people very sick and could kill. The town residents were afraid because they did not know how they could protect themselves from cholera, and at that time, a cure did not exist.

Incidentally, the property that was purchased by the governor of New York remained in the hands of the state. The state legislature turned it into a park in 1908. It was the first state park on Long Island, and it still exists today as part of the Robert Moses State Park.

EPIDEMICS IN THE 1900s

Cholera epidemics appeared at regular intervals throughout the year 1923. Many people thought that improved sanitation would have prevented the recurrence of cholera by this point. However, pandemics continued to occur sporadically. The 1961 pandemic was the result of a new **biovar** (variety of the virus), dubbed the El Tor type. This biovar does not cause as severe an infection as the classic *Vibrio cholerae* O1 and is still present to this day on six continents.

In 1992, a new **serogroup** of cholera appeared. Labeled *Serogroup 0139*, it is nearly identical to the El Tor biovar but possesses an additional layer surrounding the LPS layer called a capsule. Scientists have discovered that 22 **kilobases** of DNA are missing from chromosome 01, and a new 35 kilobase segment of DNA has been added to the new capsule genes. For the first time, there is evidence that a new strain has developed by obtaining genes from another source and incorporating them into the genes of the cholera bacillus.

As technology improved, the documentation of cholera improved as well. Throughout history, documentation has developed from vague descriptions of cholera-like diseases to clinical documentation, and finally to identification by serology (study of blood serum) and DNA technologies.

THE STUDY OF EPIDEMICS AND PANDEMICS

Before researchers can study epidemics and pandemics, they must agree on how to define death from cholera (as opposed to death from other causes). The Pan-American Health Organization defines this as "death within one week of onset of diarrhea in a person with confirmed or clinically defined cholera."[1] While not every agency agrees with this definition, there has been an international effort to describe **mortality** data, i.e., the number of people who died from a specific disease. The World Health Organization collects surveillance data about diseases from many countries. Cholera was the first disease for which this kind of international surveillance was organized.

The number of cases reported is less than the actual number of cases that occur. This is due to the fact that the definition of "case" (a person who actually has the disease) varies considerably. Because there are many causes for diarrhea, the issue is even more unclear. The **morbidity** rate (the number of cases of infection) should be confined to those cases for which there has been a positive laboratory diagnosis, but this does not always happen. Researchers believe that there are ten times more actual cases of cholera worldwide than the number of cases reported. Therefore, morbidity rate data are suspect without proper definition.

The **incidence** of infections, or new cases, with cholera is dependent on the condition of the area, the opportunities for transmitting the bacterium, and the numbers of those immune in

---

1. R. Tauxe. "Cholera" in *Bacterial Infections in Humans: Epidemiology and Control.* 3rd ed. Edited by Evans, A. and Brockman, P. New York: Plenum, 1998.

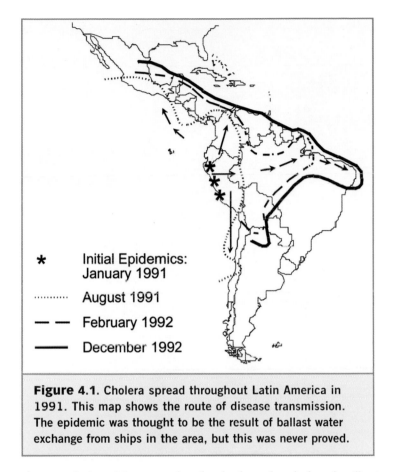

* Initial Epidemics: January 1991

.... August 1991

— — February 1992

—— December 1992

Figure 4.1. Cholera spread throughout Latin America in 1991. This map shows the route of disease transmission. The epidemic was thought to be the result of ballast water exchange from ships in the area, but this was never proved.

the population. Most people who harbor the cholera bacillus within their body do not show symptoms, and are thus labeled as **asymptomatic**. One estimate is that just two percent of new cases are severe, five percent are moderate, and 18 percent have mild symptoms. Up to 75 percent of cases are asymptomatic.[1,2]

Since such a large number of bacteria are necessary for infection, cholera is usually not transmitted without food or water contamination. Researchers have observed that caregivers usually do not become infected. This shows that sanitary

2. R. Stock. "Cholera in Africa." *African Environment Special Report* 3, International African Institute, London, England, 1976.

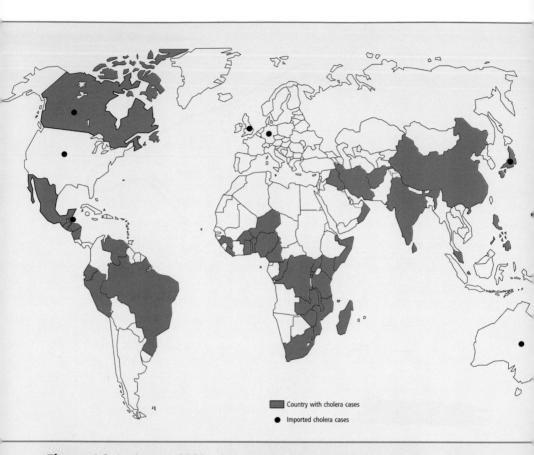

Figure 4.2. In the year 2000, cholera cases were reported in over 40 countries. The map above shows which countries had reported cholera cases and which of those had cases that were due to an outside source, such as imported contaminated food, or travel into the country by a person already infected by the disease.

precautions are important in the control of the disease. Often it is possible to trace the source of an epidemic, but not always. In one example, the Latin America epidemic of 1991 (Figure 4.1) is thought to have come from ballast water, but scientists could not prove this theory.

Scientists study the geographic distribution of disease infections because this will help them to better understand the disease itself (Figure 4.2). In 1993, the incidence of cholera was highest in Central and South America, Africa, and the sub-Asian continent (India, Pakistan, Bangladesh, and China). Cholera is a seasonal disease; its occurrence is rare in cooler months. The peak incidence in India is before the monsoon season in Calcutta and after the monsoon season in Madras (farther south). In Bangladesh, the peak season for El Tor cholera is in the fall, while the peak for the classical biotype is from December to January. Age and sex of a person have no effect on whether or not they will become infected if they do not have immunity to the disease. It has been observed that individuals with Type O blood are more likely to become infected and will have a more severe case of the disease than people with other blood types. The reason(s) for this are unknown.

Other settings where cholera occurs include religious migrations and at refugee camps due to the close proximity of all the inhabitants. Cholera is also associated with extreme poverty. Since cholera bacilli are sensitive to gastric acid, any impairment of the formation of gastric acid will increase the possibility of cholera infection. This can include stomach surgery or use of antacids or anti-ulcer medications.

CHOLERA IN THE UNITED STATES TODAY

Although rare, cases of cholera do occasionally occur in the United States (Figure 4.3). In 1991, three cases of cholera were found in Maryland. They were associated with the consumption of frozen coconut milk imported from Asia. The affected individuals had not traveled outside the United States. They had not eaten raw shellfish in the preceding month. However, all of the affected individuals had attended the same private party where they ate crabs and rice pudding with coconut milk. Unopened packages of the same brand of coconut milk (but a different shipment) which had been imported from Asia were examined. Cholera bacteria were found within the food.

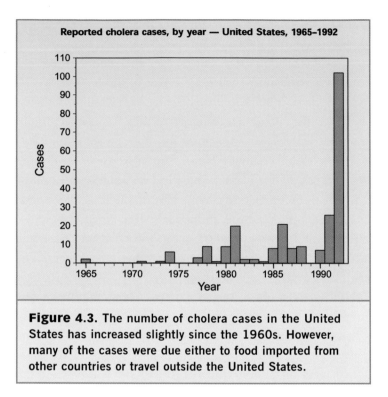

Figure 4.3. The number of cholera cases in the United States has increased slightly since the 1960s. However, many of the cases were due either to food imported from other countries or travel outside the United States.

In this same year, 16 other cases occurred in the United States. All of the individuals affected had recently traveled to ether South America or to Asia. Two of these were infected with the same biotype as those infected in Maryland from the coconut milk imported from Asia. Other outbreaks included isolation of *Vibrio cholerae* O1 from oysters in Mobile Bay, Alabama in 1991–1992.

International travel has led to an increased number of cholera cases in the United States. In 1992, about one case of cholera was being reported each week. Here is an example of such a case, as was discovered by the Connecticut Department of Health. A 43-year-old woman traveled with her two teenage daughters to Ecuador over the Christmas holidays. The mother ate raw clams and one of the daughters ate shrimp. The next evening, the mother ate cooked crab and lobster, and the same teenage daughter ate cooked crab. The other daughter ate no seafood at all during the trip. The mother had onset of vomiting, cramps, and diarrhea 16 hours after the second meal. Twelve hours later the older teenage daughter developed similar symptoms. The younger daughter did not get sick. Both the mother and the older daughter were treated with intravenous fluids and antimicrobial medication. Toxic El Tor vibrio bacteria were isolated from both individuals.

Although cholera is rare in the United States, it is still possible to contract the disease. The most common methods of transmission, especially for people residing in developed countries with good sanitation methods, is by eating contaminated seafood and/or traveling to regions where cholera is common. However, despite the few recent outbreaks, cholera is not an immediate public health problem in the United States as it is in many undeveloped countries.

RECENT DISCOVERIES

Detection of cholera bacteria has improved with modern technologies. Scientists can attach special fluorescent dyes to **monoclonal antibodies**, which bind to *Vibrio cholerae* and allow the bacteria to be visualized. DNA techniques are highly selective and allow detection of very few cells in water samples. Microorganisms that cannot be grown in the laboratory can also be isolated by utilizing special techniques.

Scientists have also discovered that cholera outbreaks are related to the El Niño effect. The El Niño phenomenon is a warming of surface waters in the Central Pacific. Recently, it has been observed that the surface temperature and the cholera case numbers in Bangladesh are correlated, and this has been confirmed using satellite remote sensing of these areas. A variety of sciences — ecology, epidemiology, oceanography, marine biology, astronomy, and medicine — are being used to gain new insights into the ways that cholera epidemics may occur and how they can be tracked.

5

Signs and Symptoms of Cholera

THE GENERAL PATTERN OF CLASSIC CHOLERA

After cholera bacilli infect and establish themselves in an individual, there is a period of time from one to three days (called the **incubation period**) before symptoms appear. The first symptoms of classic *Vibrio cholerae* infection are the rapid but painless onset of watery diarrhea and vomiting. Loss of fluids through the **stool** can be copious. As much as one liter of fluid can be lost per hour, even though it is often much less. Along with water, the patient will also lose essential salts such as sodium and potassium (Figure 5.1).

Diarrhea is caused by adherence of *Vibrio cholerae* bacteria to the **epithelium** of the upper small bowel. The microbes do not appear to invade the intestinal cells and tissues, and there is no visible damage to the mucosal cells of the intestine. In addition, the bacilli do not usually enter the blood stream, which would induce a condition known as **bacteremia**. The watery stools often contain white flecks of sloughed off tissue and white blood cells, and are referred to as "rice water stools" because of this appearance. This loss of fluid leads to an intense thirst which begins once the amount of lost fluid equals two to three percent of the patient's body weight. Severe dehydration can be prevented with rehydration therapy, discussed in more detail in Chapter 8.

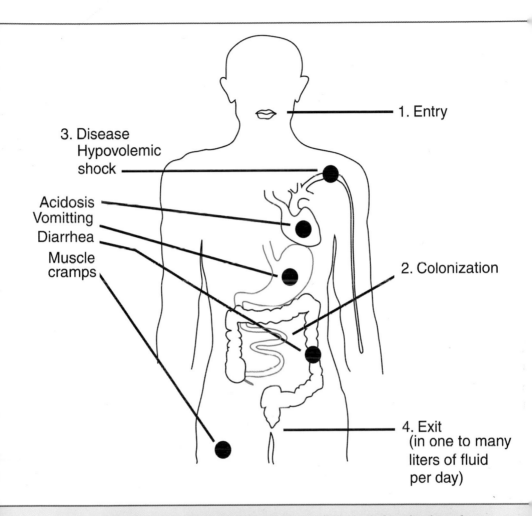

1. Entry

3. Disease
   Hypovolemic
   shock

Acidosis
Vomitting
Diarrhea
Muscle
cramps

2. Colonization

4. Exit
(in one to many
liters of fluid
per day)

Figure 5.1. Cholera affects many areas of the body from its time of entry through the mouth until it exits the body through watery diarrhea. As is shown in this diagram, after cholera enters through the mouth (location 1) it can cause hypovolemic shock, vomiting, diarrhea, and muscle cramps.

The first sign of dehydration is the loss of skin elasticity. This is due to the loss of fluid from the subcutaneous tissues (tissue right underneath the skin). The skin will lose its elasticity when five to ten percent of the patient's body weight has been lost in fluid. If one picks up a fold of skin, it does not fall quickly back into place. This is loss of **skin turgor**. This is most easily seen in healthy individuals who show loose skin over the abdomen. Wrinkling of the skin on the fingers is also commonly observed. Eyes often appear sunken as a result of loss of skin turgor, too. However, sunken eyes as a result of a loss of skin turgor may not be a sign of dehydration in starving children or in the elderly because it is also a sign of starvation.

When the amount of lost fluid reaches more than ten percent of the body weight, blood volume levels drop, specifically in the serum. This is called **hypovolemia**. There is a serious loss of fluid in the extracellular compartments of the body and also in the volume of circulating blood. The lost electrolytes, in addition to sodium and potassium, include bicarbonate and chloride. Blood pressure drops and the pulse rate may be greater than 100 beats per minute. The arm pulse is low, sometimes not even detectable. Pulses at the femoral artery in the leg region and the carotid artery in the neck region are usually still present, however. The arms and the legs become cold. The rectal temperature is often elevated. The fingers become shriveled and wrinkled, a phenomenon called "washer women's hands." The tips of the tongue and lips may be blue, the mouth is dry, and the eyes are sunken into their sockets. The voice is hoarse. Patients complain about pains and cramps in the arms and legs, and sometimes even in the muscles of the abdomen.

Breathing is labored, the rate of respiration is up to about 35 breaths per minute, and often patients breathe with deep gasps. Bowel sounds occur and they may vary from infrequent and somewhat mild to frequent and active. The abdomen is not usually tender. Patients with severe cholera usually remain conscious but occasionally coma occurs.

The loss of electrolytes in watery stools leads to other signs of cholera, if untreated. There is concentration of blood in the serum. **Oliguria**, which refers to urinating less than usual, occurs. **Acidosis**, a lowering of the pH of blood plasma, occurs as well. Acidosis is responsible for the labored and erratic breathing. Another result of hypovolemia is possible renal failure (failure of the kidneys).

Hypoglycemia, the lowering of the blood glucose levels, occurs as a complication of many diarrheal diseases, including cholera. Half of children with cholera are hypoglycemic. Forty percent of children who reach this stage of the disease will die. The reason for this complication in some but not all severe cholera patients is not known. It may reflect a difference in nutrition, fasting, or enzyme failures. There is sometimes observed edema (swelling) of lung tissue. Erratic heartbeats sometimes occur. Loss of potassium ions will cause paralysis and abdominal extension. This is most commonly seen in children. Seizures of unknown origin sometimes occur in children, also. The fetus of pregnant mothers with cholera will die about 50 percent of the time during the third trimester. Most deaths from cholera occur within the first 24 hours of infections. However, nearly all of these horrid signs and symptoms can be avoided with proper and timely treatment.

VARIOUS MANIFESTATIONS OF CHOLERA

Cases of cholera may vary in severity. Some cases are mild, and the body is able to recover in three to four days. In this case, the disease is called a **self-limiting infection**. More severe cases can result in death in 50 percent of the cases if the patients are not treated. Death is mainly the result of severe dehydration. If the patient receives proper treatment, the fatality rate is less than one percent. Most patients who recover from the disease get rid of the bacteria in their bodies in two weeks or less. However, some do not, and these people become carriers. They harbor microbes in bile ducts and shed them into their fecal material. In this way, they can supply cholera bacilli to others in the population, even though they themselves do not have symptoms of the disease.

THE HOST-PARASITE RELATIONSHIP

The relationship between a host and a parasite is a complex and delicate balancing act. A good analogy is that the host and parasite are children on a see-saw, with the host on one side and the parasite (microbe) on the other. The balance can be tipped to favor either the host or the microbe. If the microbe is particularly strong, or "virulent," or exists in particularly high numbers, it may get the upper hand, lowering the patient's resistance, thus increasing the chances of illness. If the patient has lost his ability to combat infections, the microbe is strongly favored. On the other hand, if the immune system is strong and healthy or if the patient receives treatment, the balance may be restored, the patient gets the upper hand, and the illness wanes.

Obviously this relationship is not that simple, since so many factors come into play. For instance, microbes may possess the ability to form toxins, they may have a very rapid growth rate, they may be invasive, they may avoid the **phagocytic cells** of the immune defense system, or they may be able to adhere to a specific site in the patient's tissue. Sometimes the genetic makeup of the microorganism changes and it becomes more virulent. In contrast, human factors that play a role in this relationship and may be characteristics of the host include general health, age, the quality of nutrition, the **normal flora**, (bacteria that normally reside in the host) a strong immune system, and the treatments the host might receive.

CASE STUDIES

In 2001, case reports from three patients with cholera were presented in the Centers for Disease Control and Prevention's online journal, *Emerging Infectious Diseases*.[3] It appeared that a new type of cholera had emerged. The case involved two twin boys. Both boys died despite being treated with antibiotics (penicillin and gentamicin). The first boy died within three days of his birth and *Vibrio cholera* O1 was isolated from his blood. The second boy followed the same course of the illness and died two days after his brother. The second child's blood sample was negative. The mother did not have any diarrhea and doctors were unable to collect a stool sample.

In another case, a 65-year-old woman fell ill with profuse watery diarrhea and visited a rural health center. She was fed intravenously but was not given antibiotics. Her diarrhea stopped and she was sent home. However over the next three days, she developed anuria (inability to urinate), confusion, and chills. When she was admitted to a larger hospital, she had no fever, but was dehydrated, confused, and in shock. She was given intravenous rehydration and antibiotics (chloramphenicol and gentamicin). Blood tests revealed elevated white blood cells, lowered sodium and potassium, and elevated urea. *Vibrio cholerae* was grown from her blood sample. This strain was sensitive to erythromycin, but resistant to many other antibiotics. The antibiotic therapy was changed. After treatment with erythromycin, the blood cultures, rectal swab, and urine culture were negative. She was rehydrated and had good urine output but remained in renal failure. She died 14 days after being admitted to the hospital.

---

3. Gordon, Melita A., et al. "Three Cases of Bacteremia Caused by Vibrio cholerae O1 in Blantyre, Malawi." *Emerging Infectious Diseases*, vol. 7, no 6. (2001).

Finally, a 45-year-old woman with profuse, watery diarrhea was admitted to the hospital. She was dehydrated and had no fever but had an erratic heart beat. She was given oral rehydration therapy. When her diarrhea became bloody, doctors took a culture and began antibiotic therapy. The diarrhea stopped over the next 36 hours and she could move about, but on day four she suddenly collapsed and died. After her death, *Vibrio cholerae* O1 was isolated from her blood. A stool sample was not collected.

As shown in the previous examples, not all patients suffering from cholera have the same symptoms. These cases are the first in which **bacteremia** (bacteria present in the blood) was observed. Each case was different from the others.

CHOLERA AND THE BODY

Symptoms of cholera are similar to other infections by microbes that cause diarrhea. These diseases are also caused by ingesting water, food, or any other material contaminated by the feces of a cholera victim. We will probably never know the effects of cholera throughout history.

We can speculate that impact of cholera and cholera-like infections must have been considerable in historical times. Historians have estimated that crusaders of the eleventh to thirteenth centuries were defeated by bacteria more than by the Saracens. Napoleon's soldiers retreating from Russia were decimated by infectious diseases which gave them diarrhea.

Researchers have documented that President James K. Polk died of cholera in 1849. Another death from cholera is more controversial. The Russian composer Peter Ilych Tchaikovsky (*Swan Lake, Sleeping Beauty, The Nutcracker*) died of cholera. A troubled man, some have suggested that he drank contaminated water intentionally, thus committing suicide.

One patient did not suffer from diarrhea, one suffered from only short-lived bloody diarrhea, and another suffered renal failure after treatment. These cases remain mysteries. We do not know why the same microbe will act so differently in different people, and why the bacteria that was isolated did not resemble the type of cholera bacteria that has been isolated from patients in the past. It is possible that cholera is truly an emerging infection, and the bacteria have found new ways to overcome the host and to destroy the delicate host-parasite balance.

6

The Virulence of
Vibrio cholerae

THE DEFINITION OF VIRULENCE

The **virulence** of a microorganism describes its ability to cause severe disease. A disease or the state of having a disease is a condition whereby the physiology of the body is distinct from a normal, healthy state. **Pathogenic** refers to a microorganism's ability to cause such disease symptoms. A microbe can be pathogenic but not virulent if it causes a mild form of a disease. This would be a form of the disease with less harmful or uncomfortable symptoms. General features of pathogenic or virulent microorganisms are (1) the ability to attach to host cells, (2) the ability to escape host defenses, (3) the ability to obtain essential nutrients, and (4) the ability to produce symptoms.

WHAT ABOUT THE CHOLERA VIBRIO?

Vibrio cholerae bacteria adhere to the **villi** which line the small intestine (Figures 6.1a and 6.1b). The bacteria have special filaments that recognize carbohydrate receptors on the surface of the villi. The cholera bacillus produces a toxin (abbreviated CT, for cholera toxin) which binds to cell receptors (**gangliosides**) made of the **glycolipids**. These ganglioside receptors are called G_{M1} to identify them as a specific kind of ganglioside with a known chemical structure. One part of the toxin produced by the cholera bacilli is an enzyme. When the entire toxin binds to the receptors, the enzyme portion is removed and enters the host cell. Inside the cell, CT causes an increase in a chemical called **cyclic AMP** (cAMP).

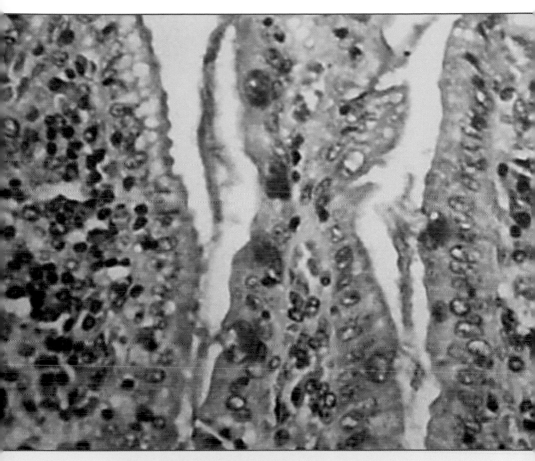

Figure 6.1a. *Vibrio cholerae* attaches to the wall of the small intestine and causes increased mucous production. This electron micrograph shows a section of the intestinal wall.

THE WORKINGS OF CYCLIC AMP IN CHOLERA BACILLI

The chemical cAMP appears in small amounts in cells in order to stimulate various proteins that respond to outside signals such as hormones. It is formed from ATP, the common energy-carrying molecule in cells, and can be quickly removed by conversion to AMP after an enzyme attack. However, while the cAMP is present, it can stimulate proteins in cells. For

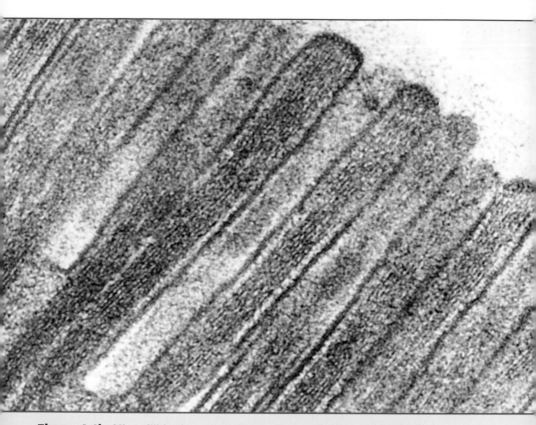

Figure 6.1b. Microvilli in the small intestine increase surface area, which is idea for nutrient absorption under normal circumstances. However, microvilli also provide an ideal place for the cholera bacilli to attach.

example, it can stimulate cells to degrade more sugars and to form more ATP. A sudden stimulus, such as the need to move rapidly in response to a threat, can request cells to supply a source of chemical energy rapidly. This is often referred to as the "fight or flight" response in animals. AMP serves to stimulate the breakdown of glycogen and the formation of glucose, which is used as a source of quick energy. In gut cells, the response to cAMP is to change ion transport.

The body must activate the enzyme **adenyl cyclase** in order to form cAMP from ATP. The cAMP is then degraded by another enzyme, **phosphodiesterase**, to form AMP. AMP can be recycled in cells to form more ATP at another time as needed. If the cAMP remains high, the cell will be stimulated to excess. The reactions can be summarized in this way:

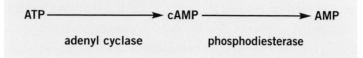

Adenyl cyclase is membrane-bound; it is activated by neighboring receptor sites that have received some signal in the form of a molecule binding to that receptor site. This changes the shape and activity of the bound adenyl cyclase so that it can form cAMP from the ATP that is usually found in most cells. Phosphodiesterase can be inhibited by chemicals that are similar to cAMP in structure. One such chemical is caffeine, a major compound in coffee. When too much caffeine is consumed, the phosphodiesterase can be blocked and cAMP accumulates. This can result it too much stimulation. That is what coffee nerves are all about!

Cyclic AMP inside intestinal cells over-stimulates the sodium pumps located in the cell membranes of intestinal cells. There is first an outpouring of sodium ions (Na^+), and then of chloride ions (Cl^-). This creates an imbalance of ions across the cell membrane. In order to correct this imbalance, water flows across the membrane from the cells into the **lumen**, the intestinal tract space. This is the source of the diarrhea in cholera infections.

WHAT OTHER PROPERTIES HELP MAKE CHOLERA BACILLI VIRULENT?

In addition to toxin, cholera bacilli have **pili**, the short hair-like appendages on bacterial cells that are similar in structure to flagella, but much shorter. They serve to help bacteria adhere to a surface, and they may be sites for the attachment of bacterial viruses in some cells. It is an important virulence factor for the cholera bacillus since it helps attach the bacteria to intestinal cells.

The cholera bacillus has a sheathed flagellum at only one end, meaning it is single-polar. This can help the microbe to escape cells that would digest it, as well as to move towards sources of nutrients. The microbe produces proteins which can clump red blood cells, **hemagglutinins**, and mucinase, an enzyme that can break down **mucin**, a protective cell material. The mucinase helps the microorganism to break down a protective layer surrounding the intestinal cells, thus aiding its penetration into a cell. The role of hemagglutinins in virulence is less clear.

THE TOXIN

Of all the virulence factors, the formation of the adhering pili and the formation of toxin are most essential for the pathogenicity of the cholera bacillus, i.e., its ability to make people ill. The toxin is essential for the major symptoms of cholera. This toxin is **oligomeric**, meaning that it is composed of several proteins. It is secreted across the outer bacterial membrane of the Gram negative cholera bacilli into the external environment which surrounds the bacterial cells. Two proteins form a structure called the A subunit. Five other proteins form portion of the toxin called the B subunit. Each protein in the B subunit is identical and forms a pentagonal (five-sided) structure with a hole in the center and is therefore referred to as a "donut." There are two parts to the A protein, subunit A_1 and subunit A_2. These are connected by a disulfide bond. Subunit A_2 is a long protein docked within the "donut" of the B portion of the proteins. It has a structure called an α-*helix* (**alpha-helix**). This structure is a coiled configuration of the protein chains; each third amino acid in the sequence is held by hydrogen bonds to the first amino acid in a chain. It is often found in proteins as part of their structural architecture. This

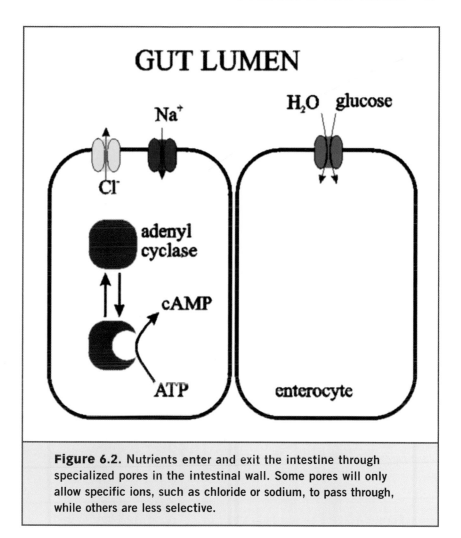

Figure 6.2. Nutrients enter and exit the intestine through specialized pores in the intestinal wall. Some pores will only allow specific ions, such as chloride or sodium, to pass through, while others are less selective.

part of the A protein anchors it to the B proteins. The A_1 subunit is potentially an enzyme once it has been freed from the A_2 protein anchor.

The B protein pentamers bind to the receptor site of the intestinal cells. A_1 is then cut off from the rest of the protein and enters into the host (intestinal) cell. It is now an enzyme. The remaining toxin proteins now enter into the cell (Figures 6.2 and 6.3).

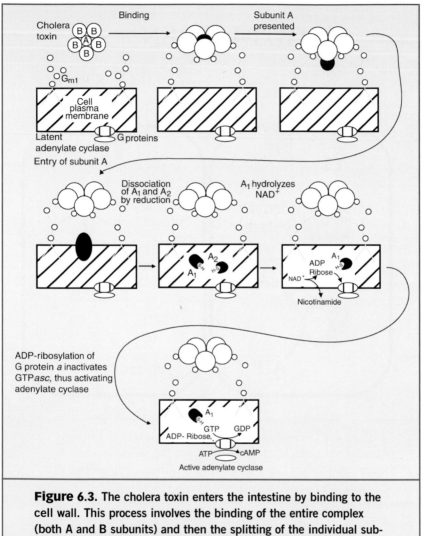

Figure 6.3. The cholera toxin enters the intestine by binding to the cell wall. This process involves the binding of the entire complex (both A and B subunits) and then the splitting of the individual subunits to form reagents that will help it cause damage to its host.

THE STRUCTURE OF THE TOXIN

The chemistry and structure of the cholera toxin are well known. The protein has a mass of 85 kilodaltons and is comprised of 755 amino acids. The A subunit is 27,234 daltons in mass, while the B subunits are 11,677 daltons each. Five of these subunits comprise the total B subunit, 58,307 daltons in mass. The entire toxin, or **holotoxin**, is 85,620 daltons. The A subunit is made of 240 amino acids. It is cut by an enzyme that attacks peptide bonds in the center of amino acid sequences in proteins (**endopeptidase**) between amino acids number 193 and 195 to form the A_1 and A_2 subunits. The A_1 protein is wedge-shaped and is enzymatic. The B protein is more stable to changes in the environment than is the A protein, which is more loosely folded.

The B proteins bind to the carbohydrate chain on the ganglioside G_{M1}. There are five carbohydrate sugars in this chain, and each one binds to a B protein. There is little change in the B protein after it is bound to the ganglioside.

THE FUNCTION OF THE TOXIN

A_1 is an enzyme. It is an ADP ribosyl transferase. The substrate of this enzyme is **NAD (nicotinamide adenine dinucleotide)**. This is a major electron carrier in cells, vital for energy metabolism. Therefore, it is produced in rather significant amounts in the cells. The A_1 enzyme splits the NAD into two portions of this molecule: nicotinamide and ADP-ribose. The ADP-ribose portion is then attached to a portion of the receptor protein on the intestinal cells, thereby altering its activity.

This receptor protein is called a G protein, because it uses **GTP** for its activity and control. The G protein is composed of three subunits called beta (β), alpha (α), and gamma (γ). After a hormone binds to a cell, this protein complex binds to GTP, and then splits into a portion composed of beta and gamma, and another portion composed of alpha and GTP. These may recombine, lose a phosphate group, then release the GDP thus formed, and return to the hormone receptor site for reuse. The alpha protein with GTP stimulates the adenyl cyclase so that cAMP is formed.

When the cholera toxin is present, it attaches the ADP-ribose from NAD to the alpha-GTP protein, preventing it from recycling by release of a phosphate group. This inactivated alpha-GTP protein promotes dissociation of the G protein complex and inactivates an enzyme that can convert GTP to GDP (GTPase). The result is that cAMP formation continues, while the ability of the cell to turn off the formation of cAMP is lost. The G protein can no longer be recycled and the formation of cAMP continues.

After toxin binding, it takes about 15 minutes before there is a rise in cAMP. This may be the time that the A protein is transported across the membrane and is split to form the free A_1 subunit. The alpha subunit of the G receptor protein binds to GTP, and this stimulates the sodium pump in gut cells. When it is inactivated by the cholera toxin, the alpha-GTP protein is stabilized while the GTPase activity decreases. The result is that the amount of cAMP increases. GTP and Mg^{++} are needed for the action of the toxin. GTP is needed on the complex, and the magnesium is required by enzymes that can synthesize GTP.

THE CHOLERA TOXIN AS A REAGENT

Since the mechanism and structure of the cholera toxin are well known, the toxin has been used as a reagent. A reagent is a substance used to test for the presence of other substances in a solution. In the case of cholera toxin, these uses exploit the ability of the B protein to bind to specific cells and to deliver a protein to those cells. If the A protein is removed and another protein substituted, then this B protein can be used as a reagent to deliver proteins other than the A_1 protein subunit to the interior of cells. It has been used to study ganglioside receptor sites, which are found in high concentration in membranes of neurons. Scientists have discovered that another protein, myelin basic protein, can be ribosylated by cholera toxin. This protein is a major part of myelin, which is found associated with nerve cells. Cholera toxin can be used to study myelin and myelin defects in nerve cells. Thus, a good understanding of this protein has made it useful for the study of other areas of the biological sciences.

Once the cholera toxin binds to gut cells, it sets in motion a chain of events which disrupts normal cell functions. Cyclic AMP is a vital intermediate for hormones to instruct cells to perform specific tasks. The control of levels of cyclic AMP in intestinal cells by cholera toxin interferes with the levels of cyclic AMP formed, as well as the control of that formation.

7

The Genome of
Vibrio cholerae

THE KNOWLEDGE PROVIDED BY AN ENTIRE GENOME

In the August 3, 2000, issue of the journal *Nature*, a research team at The Institute for Genomic Research (TIGR) in Maryland published the entire nucleic acid sequence of the genome of *Vibrio cholerae*. Determining the complete genetic code for any organisms is a major research breakthrough for understanding that organism. It offers the blueprint for all of the products that the organism can produce. More often, scientists will discover completely new genes in the process. In many cases, the functions of these genes are not yet known.

The data of the nucleic acid sequence can be examined in a variety of ways. One way is to compare sequences with those from related organisms, which may allow possible amino acid sequences of unknown proteins to be determined. An important goal is to describe the **annotated sequence** for the genome, a description of the functions for the genes of an organism. In this way, scientists can discern information about likely structural features of the proteins that can be formed by the organism. For example, some nucleic acid sequence patterns strongly indicate that a region of a protein may be folded into a α-helix structure. The nucleic acid sequence data can be examined for potential evolutionary origins of genes.

THE UNIQUENESS OF THE GENOME OF *VIBRIO CHOLERAE*

The genome of the cholera bacillus is comprised of two circular chromosomes. This is unusual, since most bacteria have a single circular chromosome. Chromosome 1 has 2,961,146 nucleic acid base pairs, and Chromosome 2 has 1,072,914 base pairs. These base pairs comprise a total of 3,885 **open reading frames** (**ORFs**). An open reading frame is a coding sequence between an **initiator** and a **terminator codon**. It is necessary to find the sequence of bases which is the site for ribosome binding and which precedes the initiator codon. Open reading frames allow scientists to locate numbers of gene groups in an organism.

HOW ARE GENES DISTRIBUTED BETWEEN THE TWO CHROMOSOMES?

On Chromosome 1, 58 percent of the 962 ORFs code for proteins that are known, and six percent code for proteins that are known but for which there are no known functions. Seventeen percent of the ORFs contain sequences similar to other known ORFs, but scientists do not yet know if cholera bacillus actually makes these gene products. Nineteen of the ORFs on Chromosome 1 code for proteins that are completely unknown.

Forty-two percent of Chromosome 2 ORFs code for known proteins, and six percent code for proteins with no known functions. Fifteen percent of Chromosome 2 sequences are similar to those of other ORFs, but products of these genes have not been observed in this microorganism to date. Thirty-eight of the ORFs of Chromosome 2 code for completely unknown gene products.

Genes required for growth and viability are mostly located on Chromosome 1, while genes coding for some ribosomal proteins are found on Chromosome 2. Chromosome 2 also codes for some metabolic pathway intermediates. Chromosome 2 has a DNA coding sequence for a segment called an **integron island**. This is a system of proteins which allows the capture of foreign genes. Genes found here include those for drug resistance, for potential virulence genes (hemagglutinin and lipoprotein), and for gene products used by plasmids which allow them to survive in host cells without damage.

Plasmids are extra-chromosomal genetic elements in bacterial cells. In some cases, DNA from the plasmid can become integrated into the DNA of the bacterial cell chromosome. Information on plasmids can give new characteristics to a bacterial cell. These may include drug resistance and enzymes for degradation of certain substances in the environment.

Chromosome 1 contains genes for DNA replication and repair, transcription, translation, cell wall biosynthesis, and a variety of metabolic pathways. Most genes that are known to be required for pathogenesis are located on Chromosome 1. Chromosome 2 contains more genes of unknown function. Many of these genes are located in the integron island of the chromosome.

The cholera toxin gene is similar in structure and function to a toxin gene from pathogenic strains of *Escherichia coli*. However, the cholera toxin can be transported outside of the bacterial cell while the toxin from *E. coli* cannot.

Researchers have suggested that Chromosome 2 was originally a large plasmid. There are plasmid-type sequences and sequences unlike those from similar bacteria located on Chromosome 2. The integron island located there is similar in sequence to those often found on plasmids. One possibility is that this early plasmid acquired genes from other species, but did not integrate those plasmid genes into the DNA of Chromosome 1. Scientists have speculated that uneven segregation at cell division could form cells with Chromosome 2, but not Chromosome 1. Such cells could not replicate, but they could have metabolic activity and be a source of viable cells that cannot be cultured in the laboratory. Such cells might form and survive within **biofilms**. Genes for regulation pathways are divided about equally between the two chromosomes.

THE RELATIONSHIP BETWEEN THE BACTERIAL VIRUS AND THE GENE FOR CHOLERA TOXIN

Certain viruses, called **bacteriophages**, infect bacteria and integrate their genetic material into that of the bacterial cell. As the bacterial DNA replicates, the integrated bacteriophage DNA is also copied. On occasion, the virus genome may be excised, or cut out, with enzymes from the bacterial DNA. The bacteriophages may then lyse (burst) bacteria that they have infected and reproduced within, so that they can release the new viruses into the environment. This can be induced by some chemicals, temperature changes, or even UV light. Viruses may transfer DNA from the bacteria it first infected into the DNA of any additional cell that the virus infects. This is one way of exchanging genetic material in bacteria, and it is called **transduction**.

The process by which virus DNA is integrated successfully into host bacterial DNA is called **lysogeny**, and the bacterial viruses engaged in this process are called **temperate** bacteriophages. If the genes from the bacteriophage introduce genes which give the new recombinant bacterium new characteristics, or *phenotypes*, this is referred to as *lysogenic conversion*, since the bacteria have been converted into a new phenotype as a result of infection and lysogeny.

Some bacteriophages are filamentous. Strands of nucleic acid are surrounded by a protein coat. These phages often do not harm the bacterial host and are lysogenic. They may bind to the host at a pilus. One such virus has been found in *Vibrio cholerae*. It is the bacteriophage CTXØ which has the genetic code for CT in its genome. This virus uses a special pilus called a toxin-regulated pilus (TCP) as its receptor on the cholera bacillus, since both the cholera toxin and the pilus are regulated by the same gene (toxR). It was observed that this bacteriophage infects *Vibrio cholerae* more often within the intestinal tract of mice than it does under conditions in the laboratory. Therefore, production

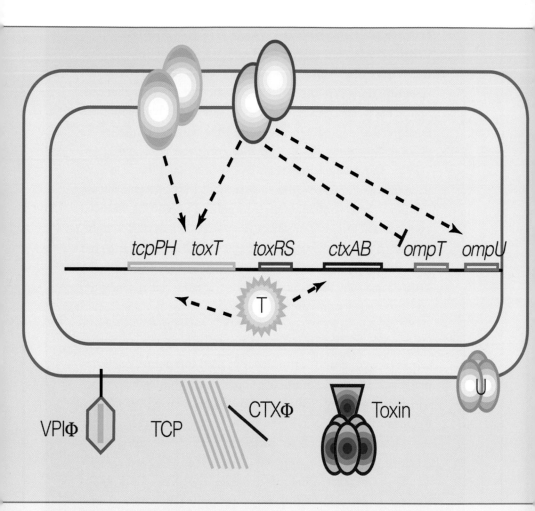

Figure 7.2. Some scientists have hypothesized about a virulent aspect to cholera transmission, as is depicted in this diagram. It is possible that the cholera bacterium uses a virus to help get inside its host cell.

of cholera toxin by *Vibrio cholerae* is a result of lysogenic conversion by phage CTXØ. It is likely that other filamentous phages may also be responsible for transfer of genetic material between different strains of bacteria. (Figure 7.1). In one sense, it may be stated that cholera is caused by a virus!

The genes involved in TCP formation reside on a **pathogenicity island** on Chromosome 1. This region also codes for other genes under control by the toxR regulatory protein and a site for phage integration. This may be the site for integration into the whole chromosome, when this region of DNA was first transferred from another bacterium to the cholera bacillus.

THE LOCATION OF THE GENE FOR CHOLERA TOXIN

The gene for cholera toxin (ctxAB) is located on Chromosome 1 within a genome for a temperate filamentous phage CTXØ. The gene cluster for the pilus necessary for entry of this filamentous bacteriophage and the regulator gene for toxR, the protein that regulates toxin production, are also located on Chromosome 1.

HORIZONTAL TRANSFER

Horizontal transfer is the process of gene transfer from bacterium to bacterium instead of transfer from bacterium to progeny (vertical transfer). In the example of the cholera bacillus, transfer is mediated by a bacterial virus. This is a source of variability in populations of this pathogenic bacterium. The new strains of cholera that emerged in 1992 resulted after acquisition of new genetic material. This tells us that horizontal gene transfer can create new strains of a **pathogen**. This could hamper the development of strains for use in **vaccine** preparations as well as in the use of antibiotics. Genes resistant to antibiotics can be transferred in this manner and thus arise in populations rapidly.

ADDITIONAL UNIQUE FEATURES
OF THE *VIBRIO CHOLERAE* GENOME

Both pathogenic and non-pathogenic strains of the cholera bacillus have gene sequences called PilD (also called VcpD). This sequence determines a protein that is required for secretion of CT as well as for the assembly of MSHA (mannose-sensitive hemagglutinin). MSHA is not a virulence factor, but it is important in the formation of **biofilms**. Biofilms are communities of bacteria in nature, and biofilms containing cholera bacilli have recently been described. The ability of the bacteria to form biofilms is important for the survival of *Vibrio cholerae* in nature. Cholera vibrio live two lifestyles: one in nature and one in a host. The PilD gene connects both lifestyles, and these are equally important for understanding both pathogenesis of the microorganism and its mode of transmission in nature.

Vibrio cholerae has an unusually large number of MCP genes. MCPs are methyl-accepting chemotaxis proteins. These proteins regulate the attraction of the microorganism to sugars, amino acids, oxygen, and other nutrients. **Chemotaxis** is the directed movement of a microorganism toward a particular chemical in its environment. (This is positive chemotaxis; negative chemotaxis is movement away from an area in the environment.) *Escherichia coli* are bacteria which have five MCP genes. *Campylobacterium jejuni*, a pathogen that causes stomach ulcers, has ten MCP genes. As a result of determining the DNA sequence of the chromosomes of this bacterium, scientists found that *Vibrio cholerae* has 43 MCP genes. These genes are distributed evenly between Chromosome 1 and Chromosome 2. The genes probably arose by gene duplication. The reason(s) for the differences in numbers is presently unclear. One possibility is that each MCP protein in the cholera bacillus is specific for a specific chemotactic chemical, unlike the MCP proteins of other bacteria which can sense more than one substrate chemical.

Another unique feature is the presence of a gene for a toxin called RTX. This toxin cross-links actin protein filaments within the cell. These protein filaments give the cell its structure, so this toxicity results in a drastically changing cell shape. This is an unexpected activity for a toxin, and any role it may have in pathogenesis is not clear at present.

The wealth of information found by revealing the genetic code of the cholera bacillus has given scientists new insight into the workings of *Vibrio cholerae*. The same information also gives scientists new questions to ponder.

8

Treatments for Cholera

Cholera killed ten percent of the population of St. Louis, Missouri in 1849. More than half of those suffering from severe diarrhea died. Nearly 150 years later, in 1991, cholera attacked more than 300,000 people in Peru, one percent of that nation's population. These people developed the severe diarrhea which accompanies this infection; however, less than one percent of the infected individuals died.

IMPROVED TREATMENT—IMPROVED CRISIS MANAGEMENT

As understanding of the bacillus has improved over the years, with it has come improved ways to treat infected individuals. Even before the cholera bacillus was discovered by Koch and was shown to be the cause of this disease, physicians recognized the importance of replacing fluids lost from the body as a result of severe diarrhea. Today, replacing fluids, as well as the important **electrolytes**, the ions dissolved in the liquids, remains the key to the treatment of cholera. At first **fluid replacement therapy**, which replaces lost body fluids, was performed by giving patients **hypertonic** (as opposed to **hypotonic**) solutions containing a higher amount of electrolytes **intravenously**. The mortality rates of cholera patients who received fluid replacement therapy dropped about 30 percent compared to those who were untreated (Figures 8.1a and 8.1b).

ADDITIONAL STEPS IN THE TREATMENT OF CHOLERA

    Step 1: Fluid replacement
    Step 2: Maintain the level of fluids in the patient
    Step 3: Treatment with antibiotics
    Step 4: Adequate nutrition

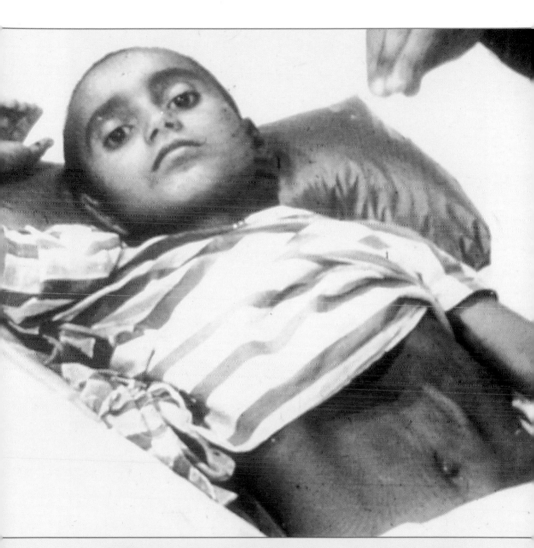

Figure 8.1a. "Folded skin" often results from extreme loss of fluids associated with cholera. The boy in the picture above has folded skin on his stomach. This happens when skin loses its elasticity, due to extreme dehydration.

FLUID REPLACEMENT

In the 1960s, scientists discovered that the transport of sodium and water was facilitated (helped) by the presence of glucose. This led to a simple, practical, safe, inexpensive, and effective

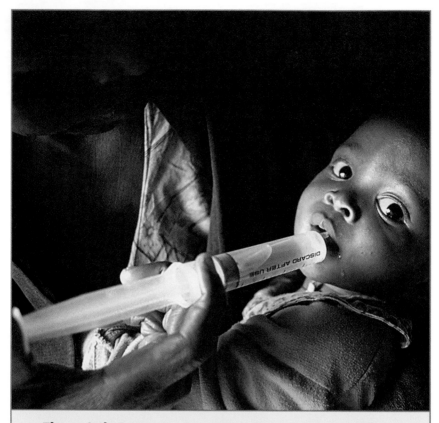

Figure 8.1b. Rehydration therapy is an important step to curing cholera. Nutrients that are lost through diarrhea must be replaced. Special mixtures of salts and electrolytes are ideal and must be constantly administered until diarrhea has stopped. The child pictured above is receiving oral rehydration therapy.

way to treat cholera called *ORT* (oral rehydration therapy). ORT is an important and valuable medical tool for treating diarrheal diseases, including cholera. The fluids are given orally, but if patients are unable to drink, they may be given fluids intravenously.

The World Health Organization (WHO) recommends a solution for ORT which contains: sodium chloride (90 mmol/liter), potassium chloride (20 mmol/liter), glucose

(111 mmol/liter), and sodium bicarbonate (30 mmol/liter) or sodium citrate (10 mmol/liter). This supplies the appropriate replacement of lost electrolytes as well as a correct pH level. These solutions are provided in sterile ORS (oral replacement solutions) packets. In emerging nations, such packets or other sources of sterile ORS may not be readily available. However, an emergency solution can be prepared using 3.5 grams of sodium chloride (about 1/2 teaspoon of table salt) and 20 grams (about 2 tablespoons) of sugar into a liter of water. These solutions have saved numerous lives and have halted epidemics.

Along with electrolytes, cholera patients will lose bicarbonate in their stools. Therefore, it is necessary to also supply an alkaline solution to replace lost bicarbonate. Originally, sodium bicarbonate was used. However, bicarbonate solutions do not keep for long periods of time, particularly if stored in hot and humid tropical climates. Sodium citrate has been found to be an excellent substitute. Scientists have compared oral replacement solutions with bicarbonate and citrate, and found them to be equally effective.

Oral rehydration solutions prepared with sucrose, which is more readily available than glucose, were also tested. Sucrose is broken down by enzymes in the intestine the body to form both fructose and glucose. However, these enzymes may not be sufficiently active when the patient has severe diarrhea. Comparison studies have shown that ORS-glucose therapy is slightly more effective than ORS-sucrose therapy.

RECENT IMPROVEMENTS OF
FLUID REPLACEMENT THERAPIES

Another approach to ORT has been to prepare solutions in which glucose is replaced by starches and proteins common to the patient's diet. The idea is that starches and proteins will be digested in the intestine, releasing glucose, amino acids, and peptides. These are all organic chemicals that should help the uptake of sodium and water. Cereals, especially rice, are commonly used and should also supply nutrients without an additional loss of fluids.

It was shown that rice-powder ORS (30 grams of rice powder per liter) was as effective as sucrose ORS. A reduction of diarrheal output can also be accomplished with this formulation. Other grains, which have been used successfully, are from wheat and maize. Unlike rice powder, the wheat preparation does not have to be cooked. These formulations are very useful and, depending on local conditions, may be used in place of glucose ORT.

At the present, there is still a need to reduce the volume output of diarrhea caused by cholera. Some of the current efforts to improve ORS formulations include the substitution of organic acids other than citrate, the use of polymers of glucose, and the use of amino acids. Some of these formulations seem promising in clinical trials, but the best ORT is the cereal-based formulations.

In emergency situations, "sugar-salt" solutions can be easily prepared from commonly available materials to use in therapy. However, this solution has no base (bicarbonate) or

CHOLERA OUTBREAKS

The World Health Organization estimates that there are about 100,000 cases of cholera each year. There were 89,714 reported cases through July 2002. This is most likely an underestimate, since many victims without access to medical care go unreported.

This fact is all the more remarkable when one realizes that cholera is an infectious disease that can be prevented.

Source: World Health Organization

potassium. A diet supplement of foods rich in potassium is recommended in these cases. These solutions are incomplete and should be used as temporary measures for treatment only.

PROPER CARE FOR THE PATIENT

Health care workers should evaluate cholera patients carefully in order to be able to determine the proper treatment. For example, caregivers must know how much fluid the patient has lost in order to determine how much needs to be replaced. Patients should also be examined for pulse rate, skin turgor, overall comfort such as nausea and vomiting, fullness of neck veins, and weight.

For patients with severe diarrhea, IV-ORT (intravenous oral replacement therapy) is preferable. Severely dehydrated patients can be rehydrated in two to four hours. The degree of dehydration in the patient determines the best rehydration therapy to use. Dehydration is rated by clinicians in four groups: (1) no dehydration, (2) mild, (3) moderate, and (4) severe dehydration. The mild category patient has lost about five percent of his body weight in fluid and may have somewhat reduced skin turgor. The moderately dehydrated patient has lost seven and a half percent of body weight, has poor skin turgor, a dry mouth and somewhat sunken eyes. Patients who have lost ten percent or more body weight are weak, somewhat unconscious, have very poor skin turgor and very sunken eyes, and have poor pulse rates. They are considered severely dehydrated.

The weight of the patient should be noted upon admission for treatment, so that weight gain from rehydration therapy can be observed. Weight can also be used to estimate the percent of dehydration. For example, an individual weighing 50 kg and who suffers from severe dehydration, will require about five liters of fluid to replace fluid loss. (50 kg x 10% = 5 kg.). A child weighing 10 kg with mild dehydration would require 500 ml (1/2 liter) of replacement fluid.

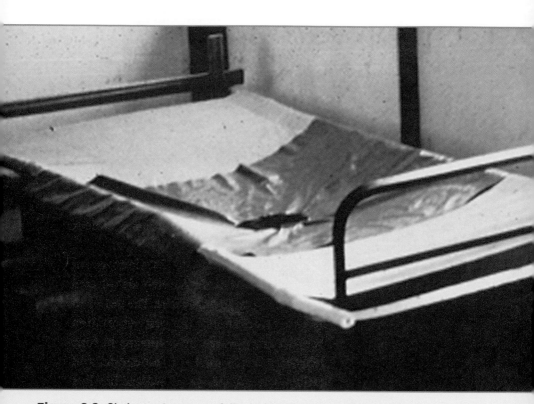

Figure 8.2. Cholera cots are specially designed so that caregivers can carefully monitor the amount of fluid a patient loses through the course of the disease. The cot contains a plastic sheet with a hole in the middle, which directs diarrhea to a bucket beneath the bed. This allows the caregiver to determine how much rehydration therapy is necessary to stabilize the patient.

STABILIZING THE PATIENT

Once fluid replacement therapy has stabilized a patient, it is necessary make sure no more fluid is lost until diarrhea ceases. This is called **maintenance therapy**. A specially-designed cot, called a **cholera cot** (Figure 8.2), may be used for this purpose. This cot has a plastic sheet under the patient. There is an opening in the cot through which the plastic sheet directs fluids lost from diarrhea to empty into a container placed below the cot. This container is calibrated so that an attendant can record the amount of fluid lost. This will provide the information needed so that the caregiver can give enough fluid to the patient to maintain proper hydration levels. A container for vomit is also provided, as patients lose fluid this way too. The cholera cot provides the information needed to keep the patient stabilized until the infection begins to wane.

THE USE OF ANTIBIOTICS

Antibiotics can reduce the intensity of diarrhea as well as its duration, although they will not cure the patient. Antibiotic treatment should begin from three to six hours after the start of fluid replacement therapy. The antibiotic tetracycline is given at a dose of 250 milligrams every six hours for up to five days.

There are problems with the use of antibiotics, howwever. People tend to expect antibiotics to be a permanent cure in all cases of infection. This is not the case for cholera. Antibiotics are expensive and may not be practical in poor nations. Antibiotics may also have side effects in many cases. These side effects may come at a time when the health of the patient is already compromised. Use of antibiotics may help only a few, and it may prolong the time in which those that have been treated can still become infected with the cholera bacillus. Since the benefits of antibiotic therapy are limited, their routine use is not recommended. However, use after maintenance therapy can hasten the healing process.

Another major public health problem is antibiotic resistance, particularly because this resistance is often *multiple resistance*. When the microbe develops resistance to several different types and kinds of antibiotics at the same time, the use of different types of antibiotics when needed in critical situations is prevented.

An example of this was experienced in 1998. Up to that time, the Indian Ocean had been free of cholera for years. Then, in January, 1998, an outbreak of cholera occurred. One coastal city and another province were surrounded by a sanitary barricade. All individuals leaving these areas were routinely given oral doxycycline (an antibiotic). Patients with severe diarrhea were also given the same antibiotic. In spite of this, cholera reached all ten provinces on the islands within ten months. A surveillance team was established, and they found that the strain of *Vibrio cholerae* there was serogroup 01, serotype Ogawa, biotype El Tor. It was resistant to trimethoprim-sulfamethoxazole, sulfonamides, trimethoprim, chloramphenical, and streptomycin as well as agent 0129, a naturally occurring chemical that normally kills cholera bacteria. Of all the strains of the cholera bacillus isolated, 55 percent were found to be resistant to tetracycline as well as the antibiotics listed above. This pattern continued as other strains were isolated at other locations on the islands.

The proportions of isolated bacteria that were resistant to tetracycline continued to climb. Therefore authorities recommended that doctors and public health officials 1) not routinely use antibiotics for cholera prevention, 2) use oral rehydration therapy for mild-to-moderate cases, and 3) use antibiotics for cases of severe cholera illnesses only. They also recommended that the areas should be continually monitored for antibiotic resistant strains, so that emergency antibiotic therapy could be used properly when needed.

Other studies have shown that the resistance genes in cholera are carried on **conjugative plasmids**, which are plasmids needed for bacteria to mate by a process called **conjugation**, bearing multiple resistance gene locations. Bacterial viruses that kill cholera bacilli have been tried as therapy. This was found not to be as useful as tetracycline treatment.

THE ROLE OF NUTRITION

The cholera patient should be given nutritious, age-appropriate food, even before the diarrhea stops. This is the final stage of treatment, and this helps the patient return to health.

Finally, scientists are attempting to develop specific medications to reduce the debilitating diarrhea. They have found that chlorpromazine and nicotinic acid are useful in this regard. However, research is still in the early stages, and the mode of action of the drugs and patient responses have not been studied thoroughly. While there will always be searches for better ways of treatment, the methods described in this chapter are the best and most widely used at present.

9

Prevention and Vaccines

CLEAN WATER—THE BEST PREVENTION

People who reside in developed nations often take clean water for granted. Yet, clean water and modern sewage treatment facilities are the main reasons that cholera is no longer a problem in nations that can afford to maintain sanitary conditions (Figure 9.1). In the United States and other nations, cholera increased as the growth of population centers increased. Even before cholera and other infectious diseases were shown to be associated with contaminated water supplies, many cities developed ways to provide clean water and sewage treatment facilities.

Modern and well maintained water treatment facilities and sewage treatment plants are the best prevention against cholera outbreaks (Figure 9.2). Where such facilities do not exist, as in many under-developed nations, water-borne infectious diseases cause problems. It is for this reason that cholera is often referred to as a disease of the poor.

Crowded cities and international travel provide other conditions for the spread of cholera. In the United States and other developed nations, there are public health agencies which oversee the maintenance of clean water and sewage treatment facilities. When a cholera case appears in the United States, prompt action by public health personnel, determination and elimination of the sources of infection, and sanitation will prevent an outbreak. This includes the proper disposal of fecal waste to halt trans-mission of the disease.

PREVENTION WITHOUT CLEAN WATER FACILITIES

Where there are no clean water facilities, careful food and water handling and prompt medical treatment can still be helpful to prevent and reduce the incidence of cholera. Boiling water, for example, will kill the cholera

Figure 9.1. Now that cholera can be easily identified, signs are used to warn people about contaminated water sources. Proper sanitation procedures, and avoiding contaminated water supplied, can greatly reduce transmission of the disease.

bacillus. However, it is not always easy or practical to sustain the boiling of all water supplies. Water is often stored in homes in poorer nations, and it may be dipped out by hand. Thus the water may be contaminated. One simple solution to this practice has been to use water containers with narrow-mouthed openings. These require pouring rather than hand scooping the water. Other efforts are the addition of chlorine to disinfect the water supply. Better attention to production of safe ice supplies is important, and this should also be monitored.

Individuals can protect themselves by thoroughly cooking food before eating it. Often, street vendors sell foods such as shellfish, which may have been caught in unsafe waters and therefore be contaminated with cholera bacilli. Providing cleaner vending carts and the means for their sanitation would be beneficial. All of these methods require the education of people in areas prone to cholera epidemics. Even then, the cholera bacillus requires few lapses in these routine types of sanitation procedures in order for it to start another round of infections.

Recently, a discovery has been made that could help control

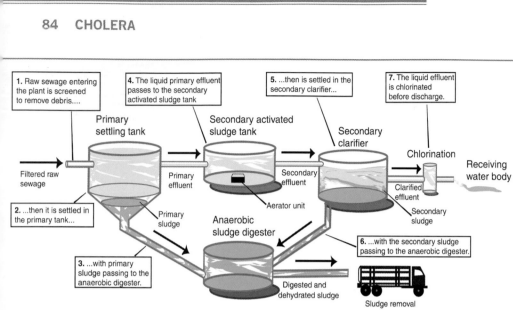

1. Raw sewage entering the plant is screened to remove debris....

4. The liquid primary effluent passes to the secondary activated sludge tank

5. ...then is settled in the secondary clarifier...

7. The liquid effluent is chlorinated before discharge.

Primary settling tank

Secondary activated sludge tank

Secondary clarifier

Chlorination

Receiving water body

Filtered raw sewage

Primary effluent

Secondary effluent

Clarified effluent

2. ...then it is settled in the primary tank...

Aerator unit

Primary sludge

Anaerobic sludge digester

Secondary sludge

6. ...with the secondary sludge passing to the anaerobic digester.

3. ...with primary sludge passing to the anaerobic digester.

Digested and dehydrated sludge

Sludge removal

Figure 9.2. Sewage treatment plants prevent contaminated water from affecting the public. Most developed nations have methods to treat drinking water. However, in countries that can not afford to do this, cholera is quite common.

cholera in poor economic areas. Dr. Rita Colwell reports that most cholera bacteria are attached to the gut of a copepod, a kind of zooplankton found in ponds, rivers, and other standing waters. These organisms, along with the cholera bacteria they carry, can be removed from water by using a simple filter made of old, much-wasted cloth used to make saris, a common dress in southern Asia. Use of this inexpensive and available material could be a breakthrough in control of cholera and other related types of microorganisms in third world countries. [4]

ADDITIONAL PRECAUTIONS

Should antibiotics be used as a **prophylactic** (preventative) measure? Studies in which family members of cholera patients are given antibiotics (20 doses of tetracycline over a five-day

---

4. Associated Press. "Old Sari Cloth Filters Cholera, Study Finds." *The New York Times.* January 13, 2003. A11.

period) show that there is a 13 percent decrease in the incidence of infection among family members. This kind of treatment may be valuable in isolated environments, such as on ships, where the infection might be contained. However, antibiotic prophylaxis will not control cholera in open environments. In addition, strains with antibiotic resistance appear when there is widespread use of antibiotic therapy (see Chapter 8). This resistance is often to multiple drugs, and thus reduces the number and different kinds of antibiotics that might have been useful for treating non-resistant cholera bacteria. The use of antibiotics also allows many people to let down their guard, wanting to believe that the antibiotic treatment is a permanent cure for the infection. They may practice good sanitation less stringently. Antibiotic treatment is not a cure and not without side effects in many cases.

IS THERE A PERMANENT CURE FOR CHOLERA?

Vaccination is the practice of introducing a foreign substance into an organism to elicit an immune response, ideally in order to obtain permanent, or at least long-lasting, protection from the foreign agent. Vaccination against the smallpox virus was demonstrated by previous exposure to cowpox, which is closely related to the human virus.

When microorganisms were identified as the causes of many infectious diseases, scientists immediately tried to make preparations of the infectious agent which would give immunity while not infecting an individual. The trick is to modify the infecting agent in such a way that it can call up a strong immune response in an individual while not causing the disease. To that end, scientists tried a number of ways to modify or **attenuate** infectious bacteria. One attempt to prepare such an attenuated form of the cholera bacillus was prepared and used as a vaccine the year after Koch identified the cholera bacillus. However, this vaccine was not successful since many people who received the inoculation had a variety of side effects. Scientists suspect that these "attenuated bacterial preparations" contained microorganisms other than the cholera bacillus.

Louis Pasteur thought that live microorganisms made the best vaccines. He encouraged a colleague to develop such a live vaccine. It had been observed that once someone survived a cholera infection, he or she was immune to reinfection. One of Pasteur's colleagues attenuated cholera bacteria by growing it at 39°C with oxygen aeration. He also prepared a more highly infectious strain by passing it through guinea pigs repeatedly. The microbe would be injected into the animals, then isolated, and then injected into other animals. In this way, a more infectious strain was selected. He injected the attenuated preparation and after a short wait, challenged the immunity of the "vaccinated" individuals who had received the attenuated bacteria by giving them a dose of the more infectious bacteria. The results were not promising because the volunteers developed many side effects. In other words, they were sicker from the vaccination than from the disease!

Other investigators tried preparing vaccines by growing cholera bacilli on agar and then heating them so that they were no longer alive. This process is called heat inactivation and is often used to attenuate bacteria. This vaccine was first tried in Japan in 1902 with limited success. Still, other researchers attempted to inactivate the cholera bacilli using bile. These preparations were called bilivaccines. When used in tablet form they provided protection for 82 percent of a population. However, this method failed because of reactions to the bile in the preparations.

It was not until the 1960s that interest was revived in the preparation of a cholera vaccine. Investigators tried using whole bacterial cells as well as the cholera toxin or components of the toxin for vaccine preparations. Strain JBK 70, deficient in both the A and B toxin subunits ($tox^{A-} tox^{B-}$) induced the formation of antibodies that kill the cholera bacillus and for this reason are called *vibriocidal antibodies.* Preparations using whole toxins or toxin B subunit induced antitoxin in the serum, but it did not last very long. Such preparations were found to induce a secretion of antibodies from intestinal cells. This meant that both whole cells and toxin preparations would be needed for an effective vaccine. Presumably, the antitoxin formed from intestinal cells prevents binding of the bacillus. The role of the vibriocidal antibodies in protection is less clear, since the microbes are rarely found in the blood stream. Preparations for vaccines containing the B subunit of the toxin as well as whole cholera vibrio cells that have been made ineffective give good protection. This preparation is given orally. Such a preparation is referred to as **synergistic**, since two preparations (the whole bacterium and the toxin-derived antigen, which induces antibody formation) give better protection together than each does when used alone.

The vibriocidal antibody induced by the vaccine for the most part reacts against the lipopolysaccharide antigen. Since both the toxin subunit proteins and the proteins for the structure of pili are controlled by the same regulatory protein (TCP-toxic co-regulated pilus), it is thought that the antibody formed in reaction to the toxin subunits prevents attachment by the pili.

METHODS AND APPROACHES TO VACCINE PREPARATION

Vaccines can be prepared from dead whole cells. They may be prepared from one strain (**monovalent**) or from more than one strain (**polyvalent**). Vaccines can also be prepared from fragments of cells, such as protein subunits of a toxin or outer membrane preparations rich in lipopolysaccharides. Toxins can be rendered into **toxoids** (toxins modified to remain antigenic but not toxic) by physical or chemical treatments. Cells may be attenuated in more traditional methods, such as treatment with aldehydes (such as formaldehyde or glutaraldehyde), alcohol, and/or heat. Mutant strains of pathogenic microorganisms lacking genes to determine known virulence factors can also be prepared. These should remain antigenic, while also remaining non-toxic. More recently, **recombinant DNA** technologies have been used to prepare such modified strains.

APPROACHES TO CHOLERA VACCINE PREPARATION

Vaccines with dead whole cells give some protection. A polyvalent preparation for cholera was effective in a little more than half of the cases. Preparations of outer membranes given orally gave a good response but were not well studied in field tests. Toxoid vaccines did not provide significant protection. B toxin subunit preparations were capable of inducing significant antibody response, but the effectiveness as a vaccine alone was not studied thoroughly. Combination oral vaccines were prepared from different sources. One, a preparation of multivalent dead whole cell preparation added to a purified B toxin protein subunit, was shown to be the best. It was effective in more than 60 percent of the time.

At first, scientists attempted to use nontoxic strains in vaccines. However, naturally occurring and chemically induced mutant strains which lacked virulence components proved disappointing. One, a strain called Texas Star-SR, lacked the ability to synthesize the A toxin subunit, but could synthesize the B subunit. It was discovered by screening mutants induced by nitrosoguanidine, a **mutagen**. While this strain was promising, the possibility of reversion of the induced and unknown mutations was a drawback. Scientists needed to look for more precise methods for preparing mutants.

New methods emerged with the advent of recombinant DNA technology. With these techniques, scientists can delete specific genes that determine the virulence properties of certain cells. They can also isolate strains which cannot grow in the intestine. The virulence genes can be removed from cholera bacilli and placed into bacteria which are otherwise rendered harmless. However, these approaches have been somewhat disappointing. For example, genetically engineered strains that cannot form either the A or B subunits of the cholera toxin, and strains that cannot form A, but can form the B subunit of the toxin, were prepared. Both induced loose stools in a significant number of cases. The strain producing the B subunit also produced a hemolysin. The role of this in pathogenicity is unknown. Scientists created a new strain, which they labeled CVD 103. It is A^-B^+ but also lacks TCP, a colonization factor for pili attachment to intestinal cells. Further, this strain was made resistant to mercury (Hg^{++}), so that it can easily be distinguished from a wild type strain of *Vibrio cholerae* 01. This strain holds promise for future vaccine research. There was mild diarrhea in two percent of the cases tested, and there was a significant increase in vibriocidal antibodies in cases vaccinated using this strain.

VACCINATIONS IN THE UNITED STATES

The best vaccine preparations available are the oral combination using multivalent dead whole vibrios and purified B protein subunit. However, these vaccines also have drawbacks. They are not as effective in younger children as in adults. The immunity is of short duration, lasting only six months in many cases. They are expensive to produce. At least two doses at regular time intervals are required (three are recommended). In many developing countries it is often impractical and difficult to get a vaccination shot just once, let alone twice.

In the United States, the Public Health Service does not require vaccination for travelers coming to the United States from cholera-infected areas. The World Health Organization does not recommend cholera vaccination for travel to or from cholera-infected regions. Vaccines present in the United States are prepared from a combination of phenol-inactivated suspensions of Inaba and Ogawa classic strains grown on agar or in broth. High risk personnel should be vaccinated, including at least one booster shot within six months of the first shot. There is no general recommendation for United States citizens or residents.

SHOULD WE BE CONCERNED?

We should be concerned about the welfare of others and about the possibilities of new cholera strains reaching the United States. An effective vaccine will help thousands around the world, a world that is now made very small because of rapid international travel.

10

Cholera in the Future

E. COLI AND CHOLERA

E. coli (*Escherichia coli*) is a microorganism very much in the news these days. Meat supplies in the United States have been recalled because of contamination, beaches have been closed because of it, and people have died from eating contaminated foods. Pathogenic strains of *E. coli* produce a toxin similar in chemical structure to the cholera toxin. It is likely that this toxin came from strains of cholera bacilli by genetic transfer. Indirectly, then, the cholera toxin is very much a medical concern in the United States.

IS CHOLERA AN EMERGING INFECTIOUS DISEASE?

An **emerging infectious disease** is one which is newly recognized, often as a result of human activity. The microorganisms in question may have been around for thousands of years without causing health problems, but may have recently infected humans. A classic example of an emerging disease is the microbe *Legionella pneumophila* which causes "Legionnaire's disease" (a type of pneumonia) after it is inhaled. This microbe was originally found in soil, where it is generally harmless. However, air conditioners with holding tanks that opened into the outside environment (as opposed to fully enclosed holding tanks) increased in usage by the 1970s. *Legionella pneumophila* microbes thrived in the holding tanks and could be spread to humans by droplets. Human beings had created the mechanism and opportunity for an increase in infections caused by this microorganism.

Could cholera become an emerging infection in developed countries? New cases have been found in the United States as a result of travel from an **endemic** area, where cases are found at a constantly low level in the population. These cases have been found to be associated with importing and eating contaminated food, and with aging or improperly maintained water purification and sewage treatment facilities. The overuse of antibiotics has created cholera (and other) bacteria that are resistant to this kind of treatment.

Scientists have recently come to understand that vibrio bacilli can enter a non-cultivatable state but still remain infectious. This means that means that water supplies which may test negative for the presence of these bacteria may, in fact, be unsafe. A new strain of cholera bacillus appeared in Bengal recently. It was shown that this strain (*Vibrio cholerae* 0139) becomes dormant within a week even at cool temperatures. New strains of cholera bacilli may be considered emerging pathogens. Future human activities such as those that promote global warming will also contribute to the possible emergence of cholera infections in areas where it has not usually been found.

THE POSSIBILITIES FOR NEW TREATMENT METHODS

Modern scientists have a renewed respect for traditional medicines used in different cultures, and this may provide opportunities for finding new medications for treatment and prevention of diseases. In Japan and China, diarrheal diseases have been controlled by herbal medicine preparations called Kampe formulations for centuries. Recently, the chemicals within these herbal medicines have been isolated and characterized. These medicines have been shown to inhibit all cholera toxin activities including ADP-ribosylation activity, the elongation of tissue culture cells, and the accumulation of fluids in gut preparations. It is suggested that the most active component of these ancient medications may be added to the latest formulation for oral replacement therapy in order to help control the severe diarrhea of cholera. This may become a future treatment for cholera.

Another novel approach uses more modern recombinant DNA technologies. The gene for determining cholera toxin has been cut out and spliced into the genes of potatoes. Mice that were fed these genetically altered potatoes became immune to cholera infection. The ability to incorporate these genes in plants may enable doctors to distribute vaccinations simply by telling their patients which foods to eat. This is another direction scientific research may take in order to improve the treatment and prevention of cholera and other infectious diseases in the future.

CHOLERA ON GENE CHIPS

Once scientists had mapped out the entire cholera genome, they could utilize the new technology of **gene chips**. To create a gene chip, scientists place tiny dots of DNA segments onto a glass plate in a regular pattern. This is referred to as a *microarray*. Next, genes from any source can be labeled (this is referred to as a probe and often contains a fluorescent or radioactive marker) and then allowed to hybridize on the microarray. Genes that hybridize to the probe will display the label. In this way, scientists can identify genes which match those of the probe (Figure 10.1). This technique has been used to compare different strains of cholera bacilli such as those found in endemic areas and those found during epidemics. A high degree of similarity was found when this technique was used, which shows that the two strains are closely related. It does appear that cholera strains that can incorporate a cluster of genes called a TCP patho-genicity island and the filamentous phage CTØ (and perhaps a few other antigenic proteins) can become a pathogen to humans. The TCP pathogenicity island is a group of genes that encode for TCP pili, a colonization factor and receptor for CTXØ (the filamentous cholera toxin phage), and toxR, an essential virulence regulation gene. These results need further testing and verification, but the methods used will enable very precise definition of pathogenicity in these microorganisms at the genetic level.

CHOLERA AND QUORUM SENSING

Scientists have shown that some bacteria communicate with each other using chemical signals. When the population density of bacteria reaches a high enough level for this communication to

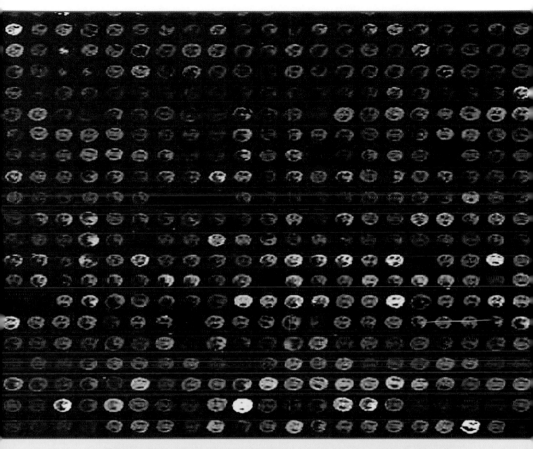

Figure 10.1. New DNA technologies have allowed scientists to better understand how cholera functions. Using a gene chip, scientists can compare genomes of different strains of *Vibrio cholerae.* Fluorescent probes are used to match the DNA of an unknown microorganism to that of the known cholera genome. The picture above is an example of a DNA microarray.

occur, chemical signals, called autoinducers, travel from one cell and bind to another. This changes the cell's behavior. In this way, the cell population monitors its own density. This process is called **quorum sensing**. Gram positive bacteria use short poly-peptides as autoinducers, while Gram negative bacteria, including the vibrio bacilli, use a chemicals including acylhomoserine lactone. Examples of behavior changes that have been observed so far include: 1) the ability to form spores, 2) the ability to form biofilms, 3) the ability to transform (to take up DNA from another microorganism and incorporate it into a cell), and 4) bioluminescence.

A marine bacterium closely related to the cholera bacillus is *Vibrio harveyi*. This microbe uses a quorum sensing system to turn on the genes which direct the formation of proteins which allow it to *luminesce*, i.e., to emit light. Scientists observed through examination of the completed genome sequence that some of the genes for this process are found in the genes of *Vibrio cholerae*. Genes for producing and responding to the quorum sensing signal were present, although genes which give the ability to luminesce were not. It was found that the quorum sensing system in the cholera bacillus is involved in controlling the expression of cholera virulence genes. However, unlike other bacteria which control virulence with quorum sensing systems, *Vibrio cholerae* repress the virulence genes. Other processes regulated by a quorum sensing system in the vibrio bacillus include motility, protease enzyme production, and the ability to form biofilms. A better understanding of the cholera bacillus quorum sensing system may someday aid in discoveries that may reduce or eliminate the virulence activities of this microorganism.

CHOLERA AND BIOTERRORISM

The Federation of American Scientists recently listed some microorganisms that may be used for biological warfare. In addition to diseases such as anthrax, plague, and the Ebola virus, cholera is on this list as well. Why might cholera be considered as an agent for biological warfare? The goals of bioterrorists are to disrupt society and to promote unrest. Killing is not necessarily, and not always, a primary goal in warfare. Creating large numbers of sick, disabled persons would sorely tax any nation's resources. Cholera could be used to contaminate unguarded water supplies and at safe distances from large populations. Massive numbers of cases would tax medical resources, possibly making the society more vulnerable to other types of attacks. Present vaccines are only about 50 percent effective, and the immunity they provide lasts less than a year, often only about six months. Antibiotics have a limited effect. In reality, water supplies in developed countries would most likely eliminate contaminating cholera microorganisms before they could harm anyone. Developed countries practice good sanitation and treat water supplies with chlorine or other halides regularly. Cholera bacilli are susceptible to these treatments. Further, water supplies are regularly monitored for fecal contamination. Public sewage areas are also treated and monitored for fecal contamination. However, should the water treatment somehow fail, cholera might survive and could make thousands very sick. Obviously, terrorist are aware of this, too.

A FINAL WORD

Cholera bacilli are part of the estimated two to three percent of all microorganisms on earth that are known to cause disease. Free-living vibrios produce no toxin. However, when in contact with human waste, the toxin is produced. There is no known function for the cholera toxin in nature. Ordinarily, these bacteria serve to recycle organic matter in waters. Toxin formation is not needed for its survival in this environment. The ability of this microorganism to form a toxin changes human behaviors. Both microbes and humans will, out of necessity, continue to share this planet. Each must adapt to the other for survival. New technologies such as gene sequencing and construction of microarrays are allowing scientists to examine the nature of the pathogenicity of *Vibrio cholerae* as never before. These human activities to control cholera will be countered by activities of *Vibrio cholerae* to adapt to its changing environment. We must remain ever vigilant.

Glossary

Acidosis—Increase of acidity in blood serum.

Adenyl cyclase—An enzyme which forms cyclic AMP from ATP.

Aerobic—In the presence of oxygen.

Agar—A semi-solid polymer made from seaweed that is used to hold nutrients that bacteria require for growth.

Alimentary canal—The connection from mouth to anus.

Alpha (α) helix—A spiral structure which gives form to some proteins.

Anaerobic—In the absence of oxygen.

Annotated sequence—A sequence of DNA for which the protein product and/or function is known.

Antibody—Proteins formed in the blood serum in response to antigens.

Antigen—A substance which induces the formation of antibodies.

Asymptomatic—The state of an infected patient in which there are no symptoms of evidence of that infection.

Attenuate—To weaken.

Bacteremia—When bacteria are present in the blood stream.

Bacteriophage—A bacterial virus.

Bile salt—A chemical formed by the gall bladder to help digest fats by emulsifying them.

Biofilm—Mixtures of microorganisms growing in a natural state.

Biotype—Strains of bacteria which are very similar and may have originated from the same strain, yet have different identifying characteristics.

Biovar—A variety of a species with shared biological properties.

Carrier—An infected individual who can transmit that infection to another individual.

Chemotaxis—Moving towards specific chemicals.

Cholera cot—A special cot with an opening which allows fluid lost in the form of diarrhea to be collected.

Clone—An identical organism.

Colony—A single microbe that has divided repeatedly to form a group of cells which are visible to the naked eye.

Conjugation—A method of bacterial recombination in which DNA is transferred from one strain to another by cell to cell contact.

Conjugative plasmids—Plasmids which can be transferred between cells by conjugation.

Counterstain—A stain used to contrast another in procedures when more than one stain is used.

Communication of disease—How a disease is spread in a population.

Cyclic AMP—A chemical involved in controlling cell metabolism.

Defecate—To eliminate solid waste.

Diarrhea—Loose or watery bowel movements.

Electrolytes—Substances dissolved in solutions and which are positively or negatively charged; for example, ions in water.

Emerging infectious disease—A newly recognized infectious disease, often a result of human activity.

Endemic—Describes a disease that is found in a particular place all year long.

Endotoxin—The lipopolysaccharide of Gram negative bacteria that is a factor in their ability to cause disease.

Epidemic—An increase in the number of disease cases above the normally expected number of cases.

Epidemiology—The study of disease transmission, incidence, and control.

Endopeptidase—An enzyme which breaks peptide bonds in the interior of a protein.

Epithelium—The outermost layer of the skin or related tissues.

Eukaryote—A cell which contains a true nucleus, (membranes surrounding the genetic material).

Facultative—Ability to live under different conditions.

Glossary

Feces — Solid waste.

Filamentous virus — A virus with a linear shape.

Fluid replacement therapy — Treatment of providing water and electrolytes to replace those that are lost as a result of infection.

Fungi (singular: **fungus**) — Eukaryotic saprophytic kingdom of organisms; also called molds.

Ganglioside — A unique type of lipid associated with cell membrane structure; glycolipids with a complex carbohydrate group.

Gene chips — Genetic material for specific traits placed on slides and which can be identified by hybridization.

Germ Theory of Disease — The theory that infectious diseases are caused by specific microorganisms.

Glycolipid — A lipid containing a carbohydrate group.

Gram stain reaction — A procedure which visualizes bacteria and determines if they retain crystal violet dye (Gram positive) or do not (Gram negative).

GTP — Guanosine triphosphate; a nucleotide.

Hemagglutination — Clumping of red blood cells.

Hemolysis — Bursting of red blood cells.

Holotoxin — A toxin including its protein and all other chemical factors.

Hypertonic — Solutions higher in electrolytes than a standard.

Hypoglycemia — Lowering of glucose in the blood.

Hypothesis — An educated guess that is testable; part of the scientific method of problem solving.

Hypotonic — Solutions lower in electrolytes when compared to a standard.

Hypovolemia — Lowering of the volume of blood.

Incidence — The number of new cases of a disease which arise over a specific period of time.

Incubation period — The time after infection and before disease symptoms first appear.

Initiator codon—The set of three bases in messenger RNA which is the first set to be translated into a polypeptide during protein synthesis.

Integron island—Genes which specify a system of proteins which allows the capture of foreign genes.

Intravenous (IV)—Inoculation into a vein.

Kilobase—One thousand nucleic acid bases.

Lipid A—A lipid in the outer membranes of Gram negative bacteria.

LPS (lipopolysaccharide)—Lipids in the outer membranes of Gram negative bacteria.

Lumen—The internal gut body cavity.

Lysogeny—Incorporation of a bacterial genome into that of its bacterial host without lysing (bursting) that host.

Maintenance therapy—Treatment to reduce immediate symptoms of a disease and to stabilize a patient.

Medium (plural: **media**)—Term to indicate the food used for growth of microorganisms in culture.

Microorganism—Life form requiring a microscope to see.

Monoclonal antibodies—Homogeneous (identical) antibodies which react against a single antigen.

Monovalent vaccine—An antigen preparation that induces the formation of antibodies against a single strain of bacteria.

Morbidity—The number of dead plus the number of infected, but living, individuals.

Mortality—The number of deaths from an infectious disease.

Motile—Ability to move, often because a microbe has flagella.

Mucin—Protein in mucous secretions many of which contain polysaccharides.

Mutagen—A chemical that can damage DNA and cause mutants to be formed.

Glossary

NAD (nicotinamide adenine dinucleotide)—A common enzyme cofactor which carries hydrogen in cells; it is key to energy generation by cells.

Normal flora—Microorganisms normally found in healthy individuals.

Oligomeric—Molecules such as proteins made up of several subunits.

Oliguria—Urinating less than usual.

ORF (open reading frame)—A DNA sequence between the initiator codon and the terminator codon.

Pandemic—A global epidemic.

Pathogenic—The ability of a microorganism to cause disease.

Pathogenicity Island—A cluster of genes which determine characters that make a microorganism able to cause disease.

Pathogen—A microbe that can cause disease.

Phagocytic cells—Cells capable of ingesting other cells and other materials.

Phosphodiesterase—An enzyme that attacks cyclic AMP (c AMP) converting it to AMP.

Pili (singular: **pillus**)—Hair-like projections from some bacteria.

Plasmid—A genetic element outside the chromosome in the cytoplasm of cells.

Polyvalent vaccine—An antigen preparation that induces the formation of antibodies against more than one strain of a microorganism.

Porin—A protein in the outer membranes of Gram negative bacteria which permits transport of materials across that membrane.

Prokaryote—A cell without a true nucleus.

Prophylactic—Preventative.

Pure culture—A population of microorganisms arising from a single cell; a clone.

Quorum sensing—The ability of cells to communicate with other cells through chemicals they produce.

Recombinant DNA—DNA formed in laboratories using DNA from more than one species.

Regulatory proteins—Proteins that function to change the production or activity of other proteins, particularly enzymes.

Sanitation—Promoting hygiene by reducing the numbers of microorganisms in a location.

Self-limiting infection—An infection that a person can ward off naturally.

Serogroup—A group of distinct microorganisms that can react with one antibody preparation.

Serotype—Strains of an organism that are distinguished by different immunological reactions.

Skin turgor—The tightness of the skin.

Slide agglutination—The clumping reaction of antigens and antibodies on a glass slide.

Stool specimens—Sample of fecal waste.

Streak plate methods—Using sterilized wire (inoculating needles) to place microbes on agar plates in order to isolate individual clones (colonies).

Synergistic—Cooperation such that combined effects are greater than that of either participant.

Temperate virus—A virus that induces lysogeny after infecting a host.

Terminator codon—The "Stop" signal in the DNA code that signals the end of a transcription.

Tissue culture—Growth of animal or plant cells, in tubes or plates, outside of the tissues they came from.

Toxoid—Modified toxin which remains antigenic but which is no longer toxic.

Transduction—Method for gene recombination in microorganisms in which a virus carries DNA between cells.

Transmission—The spread of a disease.

Vaccine—An antigenic preparation used to prevent infection by inducing formation of protective antibodies.

Villi (singular: **Villus**)—A finger-like projection of cells lining the intestinal tract.

Virulence—The ability of a pathogenic microorganism to cause severe disease.

Bibliography

Boyer, R. *Concepts in Biochemistry.* 2nd ed. Pacific Grove, CA: Brooks/Cole, 2001.

Chicago Public Library. "1849-1855, 1866-1867: Early Cholera Epidemics." Internet site: *www.chipublib.org/004chicago/disasters/early_cholera.html.*

Colwell, R. "Bacterial Death Revisited." in *Nonculturable Microorganisms in the Environment.* Colwell, R. and J. Grimes, editors. Washington, D.C.: ASM Press, 2000.

Colwell, R. "Global Climate and Infectious Disease: The Cholera Paradigm." *Science.* 274 (1996): 2025-2031.

Cronenwett, E. "Cholera and Cholera Toxin." Internet site: *http://attila.stevens-tech.edu/chembio/ecronenw/final~1.htm,* 1997.

DeWan, G. "The 1892 Cholera Panic." Suffolk Count Historical Society. Internet site: *http://www.lihistory.com/histpast/past711.htm*

DiRita, V. "Genomics Happens." *Science.* 289: (2000) 1488–1489.

Dromigny, J., O. Rakoto-Alson, D. Rajaonatahina, R. Migliani, J. Ranjalahy, and P. Mauclere, "Emergence and Rapid Spreading of Tetracycline Resistant Vibrio Cholerae Strains, Madagascar." *Emerging Infectious Diseases.* 8 (3), 2002

Dziejman, M., E. Balon, D. Boyd, C. Fraser, J. Heidelberg, and J. Mekalanos. "Comparative Genomic Analysis of *Vibrio cholerae*: Genes that Correlate with Cholera Endemic and Pandemic Disease." *Proceedings of the National Academy of Sciences, U.S.* 99 (2002): 1556–1561.

Ewald, P. *Evolution of Infectious Disease.* New York: Oxford University Press, 1994.

Federation of American Scientists. "Biological Warfare Agents (Partial List)." Internet site: *http://www.fas.org/nuke/intro/bw/agent.htm.*

Finkelstein, R. "Personal Reflections on Cholera: the Impact of Serendipity." *ASM News* 66 (2000): 663–667.

Finkelstein, R. "Cholera, *Vibrio cholerae* O1 and O139, and Other Pathogenic Vibrios." Internet site: *http://www.gsbs.utmb.edu/micro-book/ch024.htm*

Fontaine, O., S. Gore, and N. Pierce. "Rice-based Oral Rehydration Solution for Treating Diarrhea." *Nature.* 417 (2002): 642–648.

Glass, R. "Cholera and Non-cholera Vibrios." in: *Enteric Infections, Mechanisms, Manifestations and Management.* M. Farthing, and G. Keusch, editors. New York: Raven Press, 1989.

Gordon, M., A. Walsh, S. Rogerson, K. Magomer, C. Machili, J. Corkill, and A. Hart. "Three Cases of Bacteremia Caused by *Vibrio cholerae* O1 in Blantyre, Malawi." *Emerging Infectious Diseases* 7, Nov-Dec 2001. Internet site: *www.cdc.gov/ncidod/eid/vol7no6/gordon.htm*

Graves, P., J. Deeks, V. Demicheli, M. Pratt, and T. Jefferson. "Vaccines for Preventing Cholera." *The Cochrane Library.* Issue 2, 2002, Update Software, Oxford.

Heidelberg, J., J. Eisen, W. Nelson, R. Clayton, M. Gwinn, R, Dodson, D. Haft, E. Hickey, J. Peterson, L. Umayam, S. Gill, K. Nelson, T. Read, H. Tettclin, D. Richardson, M. Ermolaeva, J. Vamathevan, S. Bass, H. Qin, I. Dragoi, P. Sellers, L. McDonald, T. Utterback, R. Fleishmann, W. Nierman, O. White, S. Salzberg, H. Smith, R. Colwell, J. Mekalanos, J. Venter, C. Fraser. "DNA Sequence of Both Chromosomes of the Cholera Pathogen *Vibrio cholerae*." *Nature* 406 (2000): 477-484.

Hiss, Philip and Hans Zinsser. *A Textbook of Bacteriology.* 4th ed.. New York: Appleton, 1918.

Huq, A., I. Rivera, and R. Colwell. "Epidemiological Significance of Viable but Nonculturable Microorganisms." in: *Nonculturable Microorganisms in the Environment.* R. Colwell, and J. Grimes, editors. Washington, D.C.: ASM Press, 2000.

Holisitic-online. "Critical Biological Agents that May be Used in Bioterrorism." Internet site: *http://www.holisticonline.com.*

Keusch, G. and M. Bennish. "Cholera." in: *Textbook of Pediatric Infectious Diseases.* Vol. I. 3rd ed. R. Feigin, and J. Cherry, editors. Philadelphia: Saunders, 1981.

Levine, M. and N. Pierce. "Immunity and Vaccine Development." in: *Cholera.* D. Barua, and W. Greenough, editors. New York: Plenum, 1989.

Losick, R. and D. Kaiser. "Why and How Bacteria Communicate." *Scientific American.* 276 (1997): 68–73.

Merck Manual, Sec. 13, Ch. 157, Bacterial Diseases. Internet site: *http://merck.com/pubs/mmanual/section13/chapter157/157d.htm.*

Morbidity and Mortality Weekly Report, Communicable Disease Center, "Cholera Associated with International Travel, 1992." Internet site: *www.cdc.gov/mmwr/preview/mmwrhtml/00017594.htm.*

Morbidity and Mortality Weekly Report, Epidemiologic Notes and Reports 42 (1993): 91–93.

Morbidity and Mortality Weekly Report, Communicable Disease Center. "Cholera Associated with Imported Frozen Coconut Milk—Maryland, 1991." Internet site: *www.cdc.gov/mmwr/preview/mmwrhtml/00015726.htm.*

Morbidity and Mortality Weekly Reports, Communicable Disease Center. "Recommendation of the Immunization Practices Advisory Committee Cholera Vaccine." Internet site: *http://www.cdc.gov/mmwr/preview/mmwrhtml/00042345.htm*

Oi, H., D. Matsuura, M. Miyake, I. Takai, T. Yamamoto, M. Kubo, J. Moss, and M. Noda "Identification in Traditional Herbal Medications and Confirmation by Synthesis of Factors that Inhibit Cholera Toxin-induced Fluid Accumulation." in: *Procedings of the National Academy of Sciences, U.S.* 99 (2002): 3042–3046.

Richardson, B.W. *Snow on Cholera.* London: Hafner Publishing Company, 1965.

Salyers, A. and D. Whitt. *Microbiology, Diversity, Diseases and the Environment.* Bethesda, Md.: Fitzgerald Science Press, 2001.

Snow, J. *On the Mode of Communication of Cholera.* London: John Churchill, 1855.

Stock, R. "Cholera in Africa" *African Environment Special Report 3,* International African Institute, London, England, 1976.

Summers, J. *Soho—A History of London's Most Colourful Neighborhood.* London: Bloomsbury, 1989.

Tauxe, R. "Cholera." in: *Bacterial Infections of Humans: Epidemiology and Control.* 3rd ed. A. Evans and P. Brockman, Editors. New York: Plenum, 1998.

Waldor, M. and J. Mekalanos. "Lysogenic Conversion by a Filamentous Phage Encoding Cholera Toxin." *Science*. 272 (1996):1910–1914.

Zhu, J., M. Miller, R. Vance, M. Dziejman, B. Bassler, and J. Mekalanos. "Quorum-sensing Regulators Control Virulence Gene Expression in *Vibrio cholerae*." *Proceedings of the National Academy of Sciences U.S.* 99 (2002): 3129–3134.

Further Reading

Alcamo, E. *Fundamentals of Microbiology.* 6th ed. Boston: Jones and Bartlett, 2001.

Bannister, B., N. Begg, and S. Gillespie. *Infectious Disease.* Cambridge: Blackwell Science, 1996.

Barua, D., and W. Greenough, editors. *Cholera.* New York: Plenum Medical Book Company, 1992.

Colwell, R., and J. Grimes, editors. *Nonculturable Microorganisms in the Environment.* Washington, D.C.: ASM Press, 2000.

Evans, A., and P. Brockman, editors. *Cholera.* New York: Plenum, 1998.

Ewald, P. *Evolution of Infectious Disease.* New York. Oxford University Press, 1993.

Farthing, M. and G. Keusch, editors. *Enteric Infections, Mechanisms, Manifestations and Management.* New York: Raven Press, 1989.

Feigin, R. and J. Cherry, editors. *Textbook of Pediatric Infectious Diseases.* Vol I, 3rd ed. Philadelphia: Saunders, 1981.

Gest, H. *The World of Microbes.* San Francisco: Benjamin Cummings, 1988.

Goodwin, C., editor. *Cholera and Other Vibrios.* Melbourne, Australia: Blackwell, 1984.

Mims, C., A. Nash, and J. Stephen. *The Pathogenesis of Infectious Disease.* San Diego: Academic Press, 2001.

Mims, C., J. Playfair, I. Roitt, D. Wakelin, and R. Williams. *Medical Microbiology.* 2nd ed. Philadelphia: Mosby, 1998.

Murray, P., K. Rosenthal, G. Kobayashi, and M. Pfaller. *Medical Microbiology.* St. Louis: Mosby, 1997.

Salyers, A. and D. Whitt, *Microbiology, Disease, Diversity and the Environment.* Bethesda, Md.: Fitzgerald Science Press, 2001.

Websites

American Society for Microbiology
www.asmusa.org

Virtual Museum of Bacteria
www.bacteriamuseum.org

Family Practice Notebook
www.fpnotebook.com

Medical microbiology with pronunciation station and photo gallery
www.geocities.com/CapeCanaveral/3504/

Pictures of microorganisms by Dennis Kunkel Microscopy, Inc.
Choose "Stock Photography" at the top of the page and
search without signing-in.
www.denniskunkel.com

Online microbiology tutorials and videos
www-micro.msb.le.ac.uk/Tutorials/Tutorials.html

Dr. John Snow
www.ph.ucla.edu/epi/snow.html

Interactive simulation for discovering the origins of epidemiology
www.sph.unc.edu/courses/course_support/case_studies/JohnSnow/

World Health Organization's fact sheet on Cholera
www.who.int/inf-fd/en/fact107.html

Cholera Toxin Project at the University of Washington
www.bmsc.washington.edu/projects/toxins.html

Genetics Science Learning Center at the University of Utah
http://gslc.genetics.utah.edu

Basic paper on cholera by Dr. Elizabeth Cronenwett,
including descriptions of the toxin and treatment options.
http://attila.stevens-tech.edu/chembio/ecronenw/final~1.htm

"Bad Bug Book" from the U.S. Food and Drug Administration
http://Vm.cfsan.fda.gov/~MOW/chap7.html

Microbiology and Immunology On-line
www.med.sc.edu:85/book.immunol-sta.htm

Index

Index

Picture Credits

11: © Bettmann/Corbis

13: Hulton Archive/Getty Images

14: Courtesy Dartmouth College Rippel Electron Microscope Facility

17: Courtesy CDC/Dr. William A. Clark

20: © Richard T. Nowitz/Corbis

25: Courtesy Dartmouth College Rippel Electron Microscope Facility

29: NLM/History of Medicine

32: National Geographic

33: National Geographic

41: U.S. Department of Health/Human Services

42: Courtesy WHO

44: Courtesy MMWR

55: Courtesy CDC

56: Courtesy Dartmouth College Rippel Electron Microscope Facility

59: © Johnjoe McFadden

68: © Nature Vol 399, 1999 by MacMillan Publishers, Ltd.

74: AP photo/Cobus Bodenstein

83: AP photo/Michael Conroy

Cover: © Lester V. Bergman/Corbis

About the Author

William H. Coleman has taught microbiology to undergraduate students for more than 30 years. He earned a B.S. in Biology at Washington College and an M.S. and Ph.D. in microbiology at the University of Chicago. He was a post-doctoral fellow at the University of Colorado Health Science Center. Since then, he has been on the faculty in the College of Arts and Sciences, Department of Biology at the University of Hartford in West Hartford, Connecticut. His research has included studies on proteins from grains toxic to eukaryotic protein synthesis systems and studies of the inhibition of hormone responses by fungi. He served on the Bloomfield, Connecticut, Board of Education for ten years. He was Chair of the Department of Biology at the University of Hartford for three years. Currently, he is Associate Dean at Charter Oak State College, a public distance learning institution. He is an active member of the Microbiology Education Group of the American Society for Microbiology. He has written and presented numerous articles in both basic research in biological sciences as well as those concerning improving and instilling active learning in microbiology education. He has written study guides and test banks for several newly published texts in this field. Currently, he reviews educational materials, both written and visual, for the Education Libraries on the web site of the American Society for Microbiology. He currently resides in South Windsor, Connecticut.

About the Editor

The late **I. Edward Alcamo** was a Distinguished Teaching Professor of Microbiology at the State University of New York at Farmingdale. Alcamo studied biology at Iona College in New York and earned his M.S. and Ph.D. degrees in microbiology at St. John's University, also in New York. He taught at Farmingdale for over 30 years. In 2000, Alcamo won the Carski Award for Distinguished Teaching in Microbiology, the highest honor for microbiology teachers in the United States. He was a member of the American Society for Microbiology, the National Association of Biology Teachers, and the American Medical Writers Association. Alcamo authored numerous books on the subjects of microbiology, AIDS, and DNA technology as well as the award-winning textbook *Fundamentals of Microbiology*, now in its sixth edition.